W9-BTI-943

READING FOR THE GIFTED AND THE CREATIVE STUDENT

PAUL A. WITTY, *Editor*

INTERNATIONAL READING ASSOCIATION

Newark, Delaware 19711

Contents

Contributors

Walter B. Barbe

Highlights for Children
Honesdale, Pennsylvania

Carolyn Callahan

University of Connecticut
Storrs, Connecticut

Donald L. Cleland

University of Pittsburgh
Pittsburgh, Pennsylvania

Edith H. Grotberg

The American University
Washington, D.C.

Michael Labuda

Jersey City State College
Jersey City, New Jersey

Joan B. Nelson

University of Pittsburgh
Pittsburgh, Pennsylvania

Joseph Renzulli

University of Connecticut
Storrs, Connecticut

Paul A. Witty, Emeritus

Northwestern University
Evanston, Illinois

Foreword

As PREPARATION FOR HIS TERM in office each president of IRA reviews the committee structure and the publication efforts of the Association as a basis for planning the year ahead. When doing this I was struck by the lack of evidence of the Association's concern for gifted and creative students. It was true that the Association's meetings and publications did reflect a continuing interest in developing a love for good literature and the habits of using reading as a means of continuous personal development. This in a sense is a gifted and creative use of reading appropriate for all students. The question of how best to maximize the reading development of gifted and creative students is a different issue, however.

Reflection about this question brought to mind the long term interest and the many contributions of Paul Witty to the education of the gifted and the creative. Dr. Witty graciously (and, I should report, with his usual enthusiasm) accepted both the chairmanship of a newly organized committee on reading for the gifted and the responsibility for preparing a monograph on reading for the gifted and the creative student. This is the first product from this committee which can rightly be labeled gifted and creative in its own right. The Committee has other projects planned to further enhance the education of the gifted and creative. The Association expresses its appreciation to Dr. Witty and his committee for their contribution and looks forward to the results of their future activities.

LEO FAY
Indiana University

The International Reading Association attempts, through its publications, to provide a forum for a wide spectrum of opinion on reading. This policy permits divergent viewpoints without assuming the endorsement of the Association.

CHAPTER 1

Introduction

Paul A. Witty

RESEARCH ON the gifted student was begun during the twenties when the monumental work of L. M. Terman was initiated. Genetic studies of children of high IQ revealed much about the nature and needs of this type of gifted pupil. Recommendations were made for special education to satisfy more adequately the needs of gifted children and to help them realize more often their youthful promise. Failure to offer opportunities was particularly evident in the area of reading instruction in which studies showed a regrettable failure of schools to provide challenge and enrichment of reading experience. Although some programs were undertaken in behalf of the gifted, the amount and nature of such provisions were conspicuously inadequate. The neglect of the gifted was generally conceded during the period before 1950.

About 1950, an increase of interest in the gifted pupil transpired following the publication of Terman and Oden's *The Gifted Child Grows Up* and *The Gifted Child,* edited by Witty. The movement was accelerated, too, by the efforts of newly formed organizations such as the American Association for Gifted Children. The results of these efforts, although heartening, were meager in terms of the extent and significance of the problem. At present, the need for attention to the gifted is traceable in part to a lack of understanding by teachers and administrators of the nature and extent of the problem as well as to uncertainty concerning ways to proceed to effect improvement. The problem is accentuated, too, by the tendency in recent years of school people to focus attention on the disadvantaged, the slow-learning, and the disabled child and to neglect further the gifted child.

Another problem that still persists is found in the limited concept of the

1

gifted child held by many teachers and administrators. Commonly accepted is the view that the gifted child is the youngster of high IQ. As early as 1930, scholars began to indicate the need for a broader definition since studies showed little relationship between high IQs and various forms of creativity. It has been frequently demonstrated that one would miss many of the most creative pupils if he were to limit his selection of the gifted to children of very high IQ, a practice widely advocated and followed. Accordingly, the definition of "gifted" was expanded to include "any child whose performance in a worthwhile type of human endeavor is consistently or repeatedly remarkable." This definition is being increasingly accepted, and efforts are being made to search for the items or factors which comprise various kinds of creativity. It has been shown that gifted and creative pupils have special needs which should be recognized and cared for by appropriate procedures in every subject area. Particularly in the field of reading is there a notable neglect of the gifted despite recognition of the importance of gearing instruction to individual differences and attempting to provide for the full range of ability.

That reading programs for the gifted are few is not surprising and may be inferred by the amount of emphasis given to this topic in books on the gifted. Thus, it will be found (as pointed out in Chapter 3) that recently published books on the gifted contain very little emphasis on the importance of reading for this group. Moreover, in books addressed to teachers on instruction in reading, there is little or no mention of this topic. An examination of the voluminous literature on innovations will reveal, too, that there is almost a complete disregard of the role of reading for the gifted in most of the innovations discussed.

There are, however, some courageous teachers and administrators who, in the current crisis in education, appear to recognize the importance of the topic and are undertaking constructive programs for the gifted. Some of these efforts are reported by Barbe and Renzulli in Chapter 3 as a result of a current survey made with the assistance of specialists in state departments of education. Noteworthy in these programs is the increased recognition given to the need for a broader definition of the gifted and for emphasis on creativity and divergent responses.

This booklet is designed to offer teachers and administrators a guide for identification of gifted and creative pupils. Suggestions for providing appropriate instruction, guidance, and experience in reading are also given.

First, the nature and needs of gifted and creative pupils are delineated from scientific studies; second, an overview, as well as detailed descriptions of some outstanding programs, is given of various ways certain schools are attempting to provide opportunities in reading for the gifted; third, the role of the home in fostering development and improvement of reading for the gifted is treated; and fourth, the characteristics of the effective teacher are set forth and are accompanied by suggestions for instruction and for guidance of the gifted child's reading.

We hope that this monograph will awaken greater interest among teachers and administrators in gifted and creative students and their needs. We hope, too, that the suggestions offered herein will lead to a widespread effort on the part of administrators to undertake schoolwide programs as well as to a greater concern on the part of teachers in the regular classroom to enrich and extend opportunities for the gifted and the creative student.

CHAPTER 2

Characteristics of Gifted and Creative Pupils and Their Needs for Reading Experience

Paul A. Witty

WITH THE ADVENT of the intelligence test and its widespread use, attention in American schools was directed to the wide range of abilities within every classroom and the consequent need for adaptations and extensions of the curriculum. Efforts to care for individual differences were attempted to varying degrees in almost all schools. Special provisions were initiated for slow learning and retarded pupils, and occasional efforts were designed to enrich the experience of the gifted (*1*).

Generally accepted was the concept of the gifted child as an individual of high IQ, a conviction that has long persisted in education. The comprehensive studies of Terman, following the pioneer work of Binet, resulted in the testing of large numbers of children and youth and the assigning of IQs to various categories of ability. Children earning IQs of 130 and higher were designated as "gifted." Such children constituted about 1 percent of elementary school pupils in the early surveys, while somewhat higher percentages were later reported.

About 1920, large scale genetic investigations of the gifted were undertaken. In 1921, Terman and his associates started a search for 1,000 gifted pupils. They were able to locate about 1,500 such subjects. Then they sought to study them and to answer two questions:

1. What traits characterize these pupils?
2. What kinds of adults do they become?

Reports of these studies were published in several volumes and were summarized by Terman and Oden (*15*). In a magazine article, Terman stated that the following findings were the most significant. Children of IQ 140 and above are superior to unselected children in physical development, social adjustment, character traits, and educational attainment. The typical pupil in the group had "mastered the school subjects to a point about two grades beyond the one in which he was enrolled, some of them three or four grades beyond" (*14*). Moreover, Terman stated that not one of his findings had been disproved in many years of research. Indeed, the basic conclusions of Terman concerning the superiority of gifted children in physical and social adjustment, as well as in educational attainment, were corroborated by studies made by the present writer and others (*20*).

Genetic studies included follow-up investigations over a period of 30 years. These studies showed that the academic superiority of gifted pupils was maintained and that "the promise of youth" was realized to a conspicuous degree. Terman and Oden found that nearly 90 percent entered college and 70 percent were graduated. About one-third were given honors and approximately two-thirds continued in graduate study (*15*).

Further investigation of the gifted as young adults, as well as study of proven geniuses, convinced Terman that ". . . the genius who achieves the highest eminence is one whom intelligence tests would have identified as gifted in childhood" (*14*).

Although the results of the writer's studies of children of high IQ resembled closely the findings of Terman, he differed sharply in the interpretation of the data. He questioned whether one is justified in assuming that a high IQ may be used to predict creative behavior or the achievements of "genius." Moreover, he stressed the importance of factors such as interest, drive, opportunity, and early education in affecting the nature and extent of individual attainment.

CHARACTERISTICS OF GIFTED CHILDREN

These genetic studies have presented a clear-cut picture of the gifted child (*20*). Confirmation of the findings has led to the general acceptance of the following description of the verbally gifted child: The gifted child was found to be better developed physically than the average child of his age. He was also somewhat superior to unselected pupils in his social adjustment. He was clearly not a peculiar, social misfit.

The educational attainment of the gifted child in the elementary school was *generally* accelerated. His best achievement was in reading and language; his poorest in writing and spelling. In Witty's studies (*21*) 50 percent of the pupils in his group learned to read before they started school; almost 40 percent before they were five; and some as early as three or four years of age. Their vocabulary was remarkably accelerated; thus a ten-year old pupil said, "Flaunt means to show or display with intent to show." And Mars was defined as "a planet, God of war, also a verb."

Rapidity in learning also characterized the gifted who acquired academic skills in about half the time allotted to them. In the upper grades of the elementary school, the gifted child had mastered the curriculum to a degree two or more full grades beyond the average for his class. Although the gifted were found in all social and racial groups they were most frequently located in homes of high social and economic levels.

Certainly, these studies of gifted pupils demonstrated the value of the IQ in selecting one type of child for whom promise is great and for whom appropriate opportunities are needed. Moreover, it became abundantly clear that enrichment, such as that offered in special classes which have been provided in the elementary and in the secondary school, has proved beneficial. Yet the amount of such offerings has been, and continues to be, meager. For example, in the field of reading, disadvantaged and disabled pupils have been increasingly given special help, but rarely is such consideration accorded the gifted pupil. This tendency may readily be seen by examining the approaches and materials used in high school and college classes for reading improvement, as well as in the amount and nature of special provisions in elementary school classes.

FAILURE TO RECOGNIZE THE IMPORTANCE OF EARLY LEARNING

Terman and his associates emphasized the importance of hereditary factors in producing relatively stable IQs. Although educators mentioned the significance of opportunities for early learning, their studies dealt largely with pupils of school age after the crucial years of early childhood had passed. Recently, the importance of the early years has been brought dramatically to our attention. Thus Pines (*12*) has stated:

Millions of children are being irreparably damaged by our failure to stimulate them intellectually during their crucial years—from birth to six. Millions of others are being held back from their true potential.

Without doubt, there has been neglect of intellectual stimulation for young children in the home and in the nursery school or preschool center. It is being recognized that the provision of rich and varied experience in early childhood will increase learning ability and may heighten intelligence ratings. Some writers believe that the provision of such conditions would raise the number of superior children to be found in areas in which deprivation and disadvantage prevail. Improvement might also transpire in other groups provided similar opportunities. Thus, Hunt (*11*) has indicated that "it might become feasible to raise the average level of intelligence—by a substantial degree . . . this 'substantial degree' might be of the order of 30 points of IQ."

It has been shown that extreme environmental changes do affect IQs. No longer is the IQ looked upon as a result chiefly of hereditary factors and, hence, considered unchangeable. The pendulum has swung to an emphasis on environment, and the importance of early learning has been stressed. Accordingly, programs to improve intelligence have been proposed by several writers (*2, 5*).

Although research should be undertaken to test claims and hypotheses, it has already been shown that programs of early learning have led to remarkable attainments in reading and language proficiency.

CHILDREN WHO READ EARLY

Investigators have recently stressed the potentiality of most children for learning to read at early ages. The possibility was long ago recognized by scholars who suggested that perhaps the time which was most desirable for beginning reading instruction was age four. But opposition was great to this suggestion since most educators appeared to believe that "readiness" for reading necessitated the attainment of a mental age of six years or more. In 1966, the appearance of Durkin's study (*4*) of children who read early caused many thoughtful people to reexamine this issue. The children in a group who read early entered the first grade with superior achievement and maintained their lead over a five-year period. Notable was Durkin's description of the parents of the early readers. They were characterized by a respect for learning and its encouragement in very young children.

The parents of gifted children who read early, in the writer's studies made in the Psycho-Educational Clinic of Northwestern University, appeared to be similarly concerned about the achievement of their children during the early crucial years. These parents frequently read aloud to their children, fostered language expression, provided varied books and materials, and showed by their own behavior a profound respect for reading. Some parents encouraged their children to write, spell, or record their experiences in simple forms. Under these conditions, more than half of the gifted group learned, without undue pressure, to read before starting to school.

Several studies have revealed the possibility of children making remarkable progress in reading and language development during the preschool period. Thus, Terman (*15*) reported that one of the gifted girls in his study demonstrated on tests that she could read almost as well "at the age of twenty-five months as the average child at the end of the first grade." And one gifted boy, observed by the writer, started to read at home when he was four. He had read almost all of the books in the *Golden First Adventures in Learning* series (Western Publishing Company) before he entered kindergarten. His favorite, the *Thinking Book,* had fostered creative expression. This boy's parents not only encouraged him to read but also offered him appropriate materials. It is possible that the provision of abundant resources and conditions similar to those found in the homes of children who read early would result in increasing the number of gifted children at the time of school entrance, since reading and language proficiencies are important factors in intelligent behavior. Certainly, this is a possibility and a hope of utmost importance for the welfare of society.

READING FOR VERBALLY GIFTED PUPILS

One of the greatest needs of the verbally gifted child involves the provision of individually appropriate reading experiences from the beginning of his school entrance. If he is able to read on entering the first grade, he should be encouraged to do so from varied reading sources that are individually suitable and appealing. In every class, provision should be made and guidance offered so that the gifted pupil who knows how to read will continue to develop his reading abilities and to apply them widely.

Since some verbally gifted pupils will be able to read on entering the kindergarten, opportunities should also be provided to enable them to develop and apply their reading skills at this time.

We should recognize that reading for enjoyment is a legitimate feature of a developmental reading program for gifted children. To achieve this goal, a variety of printed materials should be made available to enable these children to find genuine satisfaction in the extension and enrichment of their interests.

The following procedure has been found helpful in guiding the reading of the gifted pupil. It requires the administration of an interest inventory to the members of an entire class. Small groups of children with common interests are identified, and reading materials of varying difficulty are made available in accord with the differences in ability within each interest group. Thus, each child may select and share his discoveries from reading material of a suitable level. In this situation, the gifted child makes his contribution from reading challenging sources of appropriate difficulty.

Extensive use of children's literature may provide further extension of interests. Gifted children, as studies have shown, usually have varied and rich interests. They collect stamps, coins, and specimens of many kinds; they frequently explore animal, bird, and plant life; they enjoy following discoveries in outer space; and in other ways reveal a large number of interests. They sometimes cultivate an interest which affords the basis of a lifelong pursuit or vocation. Their interests often grow into hobbies followed for several years. There are, of course, some gifted children whose backgrounds are impoverished and who need to be encouraged to develop and cultivate worthy interest patterns. For these children, as for others, the use of an interest inventory may yield clues of significance. These interests offer a rich resource for motivating gifted children to read widely and with deep satisfaction. When one observes the happiness children experience in reading materials associated with their strong interests, one appreciates more fully the truth of the poet John Masefield's remark, "The days that make us happy make us wise."

These procedures will prove helpful in fostering the development of effective reading in the verbally gifted. With differences in emphasis, the suggestions will prove effective also with creative pupils.

IDENTIFICATION OF THE CREATIVE PUPIL

It has become clear that the use of standard tests of intelligence will not enable one to identify the creative pupil with a high degree of success. Recognition of this fact is not new. Indeed, many years ago, the writer found that the correlation between IQ and performance judged to be highly creative was low. He suggested that the materials generally utilized in the intelligence test are not suitable to elicit original, imaginative, or creative responses. Undoubtedly, the intelligence test has helped in the identification of one kind of ability, but it will not enable one to locate creative pupils with accuracy. Several investigators have found that if one were to delimit his selection to pupils of IQ 130 plus, he would fail to include many of the most creative pupils. Accordingly, efforts have been made to develop tests of creativity. An examination of the procedures employed by investigators such as Getzels and Jackson (7) will readily reveal the complexity of giving and scoring these instruments. Although study and development of measures of creativity are highly desirable in experimental situations, the tests usually are impractical for classroom use.

Critics have stressed certain limitations in the tests of creativity and the need for caution in using them. Such criticism undoubtedly will lead to extension of the studies and clarification of important issues. Particularly needed is further study of various kinds of creativity, their measurement, and their relationships. As Guilford (9) states:

> It would be risky to conclude that because a child shows signs of creativity in art he should also be creative in mathematics or in science, or vice versa.

TECHNIQUES FOR IDENTIFYING CREATIVE PUPILS

Despite the limitations of tests of creativity, there are a number of practical approaches which are being employed advantageously to identify and encourage children whose promise of creativity is great. For example, in a study made by the writer, the remarkable film photographed by Arne Sucksdorff, *The Hunter and the Forest*, was shown in many schools throughout the United States. The film has no commentary but utilizes a musical score and the sounds of animals and birds as accompaniments.

After the pupils had seen the film, they were asked to write a commentary, a story, or a poem about it. Approximately 10 percent of the pupils wrote so effectively that their products suggested unique creative ability, as judged by three "experts." If a high IQ had been used to identify the gifted, a majority of these pupils would have been excluded. Moreover, many of the outstanding compositions were written by pupils who had not previously been observed as having unusual aptitude in writing. If additional outstanding performance corroborated this first demonstration of exceptional ability, these pupils would be considered potentially gifted in this area.

Because of such findings, the writer proposed that a potentially gifted child be considered as any child whose performance in a worthwhile type of human endeavor is repeatedly or consistently remarkable. He suggested that a search be made not only for pupils of high verbal ability but also for those of promise in mathematics and science, writing, art, music, drama, mechanical ability, and social leadership.

Scholars are increasingly recognizing the prevalence of undiscovered talent and are stressing the presence of multiple talents in children and youth. For example, Taylor (13) has described a multiple talent search by the *Utah Task Force*. He points out that there are many types of talent and indicates that if one's search is limited to a single talent area, such as communication talents, one might include about 50 percent of the pupils who would be above average. When six talent areas are employed, about 90 percent of the pupils would be above average in at least one area. This promising approach for selecting talented pupils needs to be studied further to determine its validity and practicality.

DIFFERENCES BETWEEN THE GIFTED AND THE CREATIVE

The writer has already noted some of the characteristics of gifted children who have been identified by intelligence tests. In addition to their superiority in school work and related activities, they were found to be well-adjusted socially and to get along well with their peers. Creative pupils differed markedly from the verbally gifted in these respects. It should be observed, however, that verbally gifted pupils also exhibit almost every type of social maladjustment; but the incidence is not frequent when compared with the number in the general population. Moreover, it is much lower than in groups of creative pupils. Torrance (*18*) has stressed the problems in adjustment faced by creative pupils. He points out that when an individual has a *new* idea, he becomes immediately a minority of one. The independence of mind of the creative pupil implies a nonconformity to group pressures, a condition which often leads to adjustment problems. Torrance states that "In no group thus far studied have we failed to find relatively clear evidence of the operation of pressures against the most creative members of the group . . ." (*18*). Thus, many highly creative pupils may become "disturbing elements" in the classroom.

The findings of Torrance are supported by a remarkable study of talented persons made by Victor and Mildred G. Goertzel (*8*). These authors chose 400 persons acknowledged as "eminent" by a high frequency of biographies currently written about them. After studying the childhood of the subjects, the Goertzels reported that almost all were early readers. Moreover, they were original in their thinking but impatient with routine. They were often rejected by their peers. Three out of five experienced serious problems in school. The Goertzels conclude:

> Now as in the days of the Four Hundred, the child who is both intelligent and creative remains society's most valuable resource. When we learn to work with him instead of against him, his talents may reward us in ways beyond our ability to imagine.

It may readily be seen that the teacher has an unusual opportunity to help the creative pupil meet personal and social problems through reading. Not only will wide reading enable him to gain information to satisfy and extend his interests but it may also aid him to meet personal and social problems with greater success as well as to build an appropriate ideal of self

(*19*). Following are suggestions for satisfying some of the needs of the gifted and the creative pupil through reading.

READING FOR THE GIFTED AND THE CREATIVE

Earlier the writer stressed some needs of one type of the gifted, namely, pupils of high verbal ability. The following suggestions apply not only to such pupils but also to others who display various kinds of creativity. Both types are referred to as "gifted" in the following discussion.

Provisions are needed for a widespread installation of programs for early education. Such programs should prove beneficial for most children since the early years constitute the period when learning is most rapid. Abilities of many kinds may be nourished through offering varied early opportunities for acquiring information and skills. It has been suggested that the early years may prove to be the optimal time to initiate instruction in reading and related language acquisitions. Creativity may also be cultivated profitably during these crucial years. There is a pressing need for establishing centers for early learning throughout our country in which reading will have high priority.

It has been shown that many gifted children can read on entering the kindergarten and the first grade. At this time, they should be given opportunities to develop and use widely their reading skills. During the primary grades, routine basal reading instruction should be replaced by a balanced program adapted to differences in abilities and interests.

The interests of gifted pupils should be employed to motivate reading. The teacher who advocates individualized reading may help pupils to satisfy their interests by making accessible a wide assortment of reading materials. Teachers who follow the language-experience approach often make an important contribution, too, by leading children to prepare, read, and share their own "books." In the classes of skilled teachers, the interests and abilities of gifted pupils develop rapidly. By the time they reach the fourth grade, they will typically have become avid readers. Effective teachers provide additional motivation through associating reading with carefully selected films, filmstrips, and TV programs. Teachers and librarians can work effectively together in behalf of the gifted. Sometimes, they use interest inventories as a basis for the suggestion of more appropriate and diversified reading.

Several writers have stressed the gifted child's need for added experience in critical reading throughout the intermediate grades and the high school. And others have emphasized his need for reading experience to help him meet his personal and social problems. The reading of narratives and biographies may help gifted pupils to deal more successfully with problems as they arise. Although pupils may not be helped by reading alone, such reading may prove beneficial, particularly if it is associated with discussion and related experiences. In many cases it has been remarkably effective. For example, *Amos Fortune: Free Man* by Elizabeth Yates provided the basis for a wholesome identification of a discouraged boy with the central character in the story who met successfully problems similar to his own difficulties. The influence of several biographies about Thomas Jefferson inspired a gifted child to remark, "Everyone should read about the many things this man did to make his country great. Each of us ought to be able to do something, especially when we realize what one man was able to do."

A gifted boy, on his way to becoming a competent historian, read many of the books in the *Landmark* and the *World Landmark* series and critically analyzed their authenticity by comparing them with other biographies. He was greatly influenced by Genevieve Foster's association of the times with each historical character's life. After he had read widely, the boy stated that he was convinced that biography is "our only real history."

Gifted children should be encouraged to enjoy poetry, an area of reading sometimes neglected by them. They should be given opportunities to write poetry, too. Their products are often superior; in addition, their writing sometimes reveals pressing individual problems or needs. From the first, children should have access to collections of poetry. Very young children in our studies were found to enjoy the writing of Dr. Seuss and A. A. Milne. In the junior and senior high schools, students liked the verse of Ogden Nash, Arthur Guiterman, and many other poets, such as Millay, Frost, Dickinson, and Sandburg.

Gifted children should have opportunities to enjoy humorous presentations. Some books depict hilarious situations which gifted pupils have found engaging. The humor of Robert McCloskey's *Homer Price* was almost universally appreciated by these elementary school pupils. Gifted pupils will seek out and enjoy other humorous books if they are given an opportunity to read extensively. There will be a wide range of choices, but favorites will probably include the Seuss books, Disney illustrated publications, *Mr. Popper's Penguins* by Richard and Florence Atwater, the appealing nonsense in Walter R. Brooks' *Freddy Books*, and the comical adventures of Hugh Lofting's *Dr. Doolittle*.

The guidance of reading continues to be a responsibility of the teacher in the high school. In order to offer assistance to gifted pupils who are in need of improved reading skills, the teacher should first ascertain the pupil's reading status. Testing should proceed periodically throughout the elementary and secondary school. Specific plans for building skills should then be worked out for each pupil in accord with his interests and needs. Gifted pupils often need experience in reading critically throughout their school careers. They need to examine and evaluate the meanings and possible interpretations of printed materials of various kinds. They should be encouraged also to read widely and to enjoy reading.

It is unfortunate that reading improvement courses for the high school student seldom stress critical reading and creative response. Too much attention is usually allotted to speed reading or to repeating facts rather than to examining the authenticity, implications, and significance of printed materials.

Scholars stress the fact that a great stimulation would be given to the education of the gifted, as well as to education generally, by a widespread inauguration of programs in creative reading. Creative reading may be regarded as the highest and most neglected type of reading. We may think of one type of reading as simple comprehension involving accurate identification of words and other thought units. For this type of reading, emphasis on skills such as getting the central thought of a passage or noting details is appropriate. These responses are to a marked degree *convergent* in nature. Only to a small degree do they extend beyond the facts presented and become *divergent* in nature. In creative reading, *divergent* response is stressed. Relationships among facts are examined, and interpretations are drawn. As Torrence (*17*) states,

> When a person reads creatively, he is sensitive to problems and possibilities in whatever he reads. He makes himself aware of the gaps in knowledge, the unsolved problems, the missing elements, things that are incomplete or out of focus. To resolve this tension, so important in the creative thinking process, the creative reader sees new relationships, creates new combinations, synthesizes relatively unrelated elements into a coherent whole, redefines or transforms certain pieces of information to discover new uses, and builds onto what is known.

THE ROLE OF THE TEACHER

The teacher who guides the reading of gifted children will need to become informed about the development of children and youth and should be skilled in using child study techniques, such as the interest inventory. The teacher should also become thoroughly acquainted with literature for children and youth and should work closely with parents and librarians in obtaining suitable and varied materials to satisfy the interests and meet the needs of gifted and creative pupils. The teacher may be helped by the study of anthologies of literature for children and youth and by the examination of booklists. These teachers should read widely and communicate to pupils their enthusiasm and pleasure in reading.

Teachers of the gifted and creative student should be broadly informed about poetry. Some teachers are introducing gifted pupils to poetry from collections. To stimulate an interest in poetry, many others are using recordings, and some are becoming skilled in reading aloud favorite selections to foster enjoyment of poetry. Further enjoyment of poetry may be engendered by encouraging children to write poetry. Proficiency in telling stories is also a characteristic of the stimulating teacher.

In recent years, there has been a prolonged search for *the* most efficient method to teach beginning reading. Repeatedly, it has been found that successful instruction accompanies the use of varied methods and that no single method is conspicuously superior to other methods.

Occasionally, a glimpse of the recognition of the importance of factors other than "methods" is found in a comparative study. The writer believes that failure to consider the characteristics and practices of the teacher is a great weakness in the study of "methods." His belief is substantiated by Chall's most perceptive report (*3*) of her impression based on her observations of more than ten different classes and teachers using various methods of reading instruction:

> How interested pupils are in learning to read, I concluded, is not determined by what method or set of materials they are using. I saw excitement, enthusiasm, and general interest exhibited in classes using every reading program. I also saw children respond to each with listlessness, apathy, boredom, restlessness.
>
> Generally, it is what the teacher did with the method, the materials, and the children rather than the method itself that seemed to make the difference.

SUMMARY

Few schools have comprehensive reading programs for gifted and creative students. There is a neglect of such pupils as attention and opportunities are increasingly offered to the "disadvantaged" and other exceptional groups. There are, of course, many gifted pupils among the disadvantaged who should be identified and helped to realize their potentialities. Reading offers for all gifted and creative pupils an avenue by which potentialities may be more fully realized and satisfactions may be heightened.

In this chapter, the writer has defined and described gifted and creative students and has indicated some of their most insistent needs for reading instruction and related experiences. The need for more adequate teacher-training is stressed. In the following chapter, brief descriptions will be given of reading and language programs which are being developed and employed to satisfy these needs. It will be noted that diversity is the chief characteristic of these programs and that theory and practice vary widely from school to school. It is notable also that the work of Guilford (*10*) on the structure of intellect has deeply influenced the development of several programs which emphasize divergent thinking as well as evaluation. The variety and richness of the practices should enable the teacher to find suggestions which can be employed rewardingly in fostering thinking skills so frequently neglected in the past in reading and language instruction.

REFERENCES

1. Barbe, Walter B. *Psychology and Education of the Gifted: Selected Readings.* New York: Appleton-Century-Crofts, 1965.
2. Beck, Joan. *How to Raise a Brighter Child.* New York: Trident Press, 1967.
3. Chall, Jeanne S. *Learning to Read: The Great Debate.* New York: McGraw-Hill, 1967.
4. Durkin, Dolores. *Children Who Read Early.* New York: Teachers College Press, Columbia University, 1966.
5. Engelmann, Siegfried, and Therese Engelmann. *Give Your Child a Superior Mind.* New York: Simon and Schuster, 1966.
6. Gallagher, James J. *Teaching the Gifted Child.* Boston: Allyn and Bacon, 1964.
7. Getzels, J. W., and P. W. Jackson. *Creativity and Intelligence.* New York: John Wiley and Sons, 1962.
8. Goertzel, Victor, and Mildred G. Goertzel. *Cradles of Eminence.* Boston: Little, Brown, 1962.
9. Guilford, J. P. "Potentiality for Creativity," *Gifted Child Quarterly,* 6 (Autumn 1962).
10. Guilford, J. P. "Structure of Intellect," *Psychological Bulletin,* 53, 1956.
11. Hunt, J. McV. *Intelligence and Experience.* New York: Ronald Press, 1961.
12. Pines, Maya. *Revolution in Learning—The Years from Birth to Six.* New York: Harper and Row, 1967.
13. Taylor, Calvin W. "Multiple Talent Search," *The Instructor,* April 1968.
14. Terman, Lewis M. "The Discovery and Encouragement of Exceptional Talent," *American Psychologist,* 9 (June 1954).
15. Terman, Lewis M., and Melita H. Oden. *The Gifted Child Grows Up.* Stanford, California: Stanford University Press, 1947.

16. Torrance, E. Paul. "Explorations in Creative Thinking," *Education,* 81 (December 1960).
17. Torrance, E. Paul. *Gifted Children in the Classroom.* New York: Macmillan, 1965.
18. Torrance, E. Paul. "Problems of Highly Creative Children," *Gifted Child Quarterly,* 5 (Summer 1961).
19. Witty, Paul A. "Reading for the Gifted," in J. Allen Figurel (Ed.), *Reading and Realism,* 1968 Proceedings, Volume 13, Part 1. Newark, Delaware: International Reading Association, 1969.
20. Witty, Paul A. (Ed.). *The Gifted Child.* Boston: D. C. Heath, 1951.
21. Witty, Paul A. "Who Are the Gifted?" *Education for the Gifted,* Fifty-seventh Yearbook of the National Society for the Study of Education, Part II. Chicago: University of Chicago Press, 1958.

CHAPTER 3

Innovative Reading Programs for the Gifted and Creative

Walter B. Barbe and Joseph Renzulli
with the assistance of
Michael Labuda and Carolyn Callahan

PLANNED DIFFERENTIATION of reading instruction is necessary if the gifted and creative are to receive the type of education they both need and deserve. The past decade has included increased interest in, and support of, differentiated education. Characteristic of the change has been greater recognition of individual differences and of the need for suitable provision for differences. Improvement of education for all has been emphasized, with recognition that differentiated educational opportunities are necessary. As more appropriate opportunities have been made available, the need for specialized programs for children at the extremes of the intellectual range has been noted; and provisions have been made to varying degrees.

The terms "gifted" and "creative" are interpreted broadly in this chapter, meaning those individuals who have demonstrated superior ability as well as those individuals who have the potential for such performance. Although tests of intelligence and of creativity have some value, their limitations in identifying gifted and creative pupils should be recognized; a plea should be made that the terms "gifted" and "creative" be as inclusive as possible. The language arts program offers an opportunity for many potentially gifted and creative youngsters to perform in superior ways which cannot be anticipated from their test scores. In fact, the language arts program with its diversity of activity and encompassing range of interests and skills offers the teacher the opportunity to serve as the talent scout, always seeking to identify special gifts within individual children.

The term "reading" is intimately related to the entire range of the language arts curriculum. This chapter, in dealing with reading programs, is concerned with both the process and the results of reading: with both how the child reads and what he reads (*18*). Therefore, we have included programs which are concerned with teaching the gifted and creative child how to read, as well as literature and humanities programs which deal more with the use he makes of acquired reading skills.

There is evidence that too little attention has been directed toward reading and reading programs for the gifted. Tisdall (*12*) reviewed fifteen books on the education of the gifted and found that nine of the books made no reference to reading either in the table of contents or in the index. Of the remaining six books, three devoted no more than five pages each to the subject of reading, two devoted between five and ten pages, and only one contained a major-length discussion on this important subject. Tisdall concluded that the material on reading represented a total of approximately 1.35 percent of the total content of these fifteen books on the gifted.

Historically, there has been a continuing, if minimal, amount of interest in the gifted child and his reading. Terman (*11*) early studied the reading of gifted children, as did Witty (*13*). Witty's interest has continued as he reported periodically on the gifted and his reading (*17*). Strang (*9*) and Barbe (*1*), also, have written on this topic. Considering the importance of reading to the gifted, the paucity of interest is difficult to understand.

Specific programs that focus on reading, creativity, language arts, and the humanities have been identified by means of a survey which was carried out with the cooperation of state department of education consultants in reading and education of the gifted. Consultants from 35 states reported the names of 77 school districts throughout the country where programing for gifted and creative youngsters was in operation. Follow-up letters requesting descriptive information from these districts yielded 49 replies that ranged from one-page general descriptions to complete copies of curricular materials. Additional information relating to current programs was obtained from a review of articles in professional journals and International Reading Association publications.

The programs described have been classified into four groups according to grade level. Many of the reported activities cut across traditional patterns of school organization; a number of school districts indicated that comprehensive programing for gifted youngsters spans the entire school program from the primary grades through the senior high school. No attempt has been made in the present chapter to list all of the programs or to describe in detail many of the excellent practices that were reported in the survey. Rather, an attempt has been made to describe representative and innovative practices that are illustrative of the ways in which schools are providing for their gifted and creative students through reading and related areas.

A large vocabulary, high level of reading ability, and a wide variety of reading interests are characteristics of those schoolaged children identified as gifted (*3*). It is, therefore, important that we be certain that the school reading program is effectively developing each child to the limit of his abilities; for if we fail, there will be many potentially gifted and creative students whose abilities will never be identified or nurtured.

Of overall importance is the recognition that "a desirable reading program recognizes various needs for reading" (*14*). The reading needs of the gifted and creative differ in some respects from those of other groups; indeed, needs may be different for each child within each group. This condition can only be resolved by individualization of instruction, which includes differentiation of methods, materials, and means of evaluating and reporting progress.

Tisdall (*12*) identified both general and specific needs of the gifted which must be met through their reading program. Twelve specific needs are stressed.

1. Differentiation of instruction is imperative.
2. Regular and careful evaluation of the child's reading ability and achievement is called for.
3. Proper grouping for instruction is needed.
4. The readiness program must be adapted to the child and his needs.
5. The gifted pupil needs to be actively involved in reading instruction.
6. Differentiation of reading style according to the type and purpose of material read is necessary.
7. An ever-increasing range of reading material must be made available to the gifted pupil.
8. The gifted child needs guidance in critical reading.
9. Intellectually superior students must be challenged if learning is to take place and interest in learning maintained.
10. The gifted child needs continuity in reading instruction throughout his school career.
11. The gifted child needs and can obtain a realization of self-fulfillment through reading.
12. Gifted children need superior teachers.

The foregoing list is similar to Witty's more extended treatment found in Chapter 2 of this monograph. It must be remembered that a primary goal of reading instruction is the development of permanent interest in reading and the habit of wide reading. The mastery of the techniques of reading affords only a means of achieving a goal and must not become an end in itself. Particularly for the gifted and creative student, the practice of emphasizing decoding, at the expense of meaning and enjoyment, is regrettable.

PROGRAMS IN PRIMARY GRADES

Many of the practices reported for gifted students at the primary level are aimed at providing enrichment experiences for youngsters who have already mastered the basic skills of their respective grade levels. The primary-level gifted youngster who has not experienced any difficulty in beginning reading usually masters the basic skills in far less time than that which is required for the majority of other youngsters. Unless appropriate steps are taken, he may become bored with the activities of less advanced readers. In a number of schools, imaginative teachers are capitalizing upon this "extra" time by providing advanced primary readers with learning experiences and materials that are commensurate with their ability levels and more mature interests. These programs focus on a variety of objectives and activities; and although a detailed description of each school's efforts is beyond the scope of the present chapter, a brief portrayal of selected programs will provide the reader with an overview of current practices for superior primary-level students.

At the Edwardsville Community Schools in Illinois, special efforts are made to identify the intellectual processes and thinking strategies found in a comprehensive list of supplementary readers, records, and films. Through the use of these materials, primary grade youngsters are given opportunities to combine reading, listening, and viewing experiences and to practice creative thinking by producing a flow and variety of unusual ideas. A theoretical model that consists of eight divergent education processes and twenty-three learning strategies is used to guide teachers in the development of imagination, curiosity, originality, and the willingness to take risks. The strategies include visualization skills, exploring the mystery of things, thinking of possibilities, intuitive expressions, provocative questions, skills of search, and examples of chance.

Many bright students at the primary level enjoy the challenge of locating the origin and meaning of new words. Bigaj (5) has suggested that the gifted pupil's interest in the historical development of language can be fostered through the use of trade books such as Laird's *Tree of Language* (World Publishing Company), Krauss' *Pop-Up Sound Alikes* (Random House), and Rand's *Sparkle and Spin: A Book About Words* (Harcourt, Brace and World). Exploring the meaning of new words (including foreign language words) through the preparation of word-and-picture displays is an enjoyable group or individual activity that can be used to promote both vocabulary development and research skills in the primary grade pupils.

A popular approach for superior readers at the primary level is to integrate mythology and folklore with oral, written, and artistic expression. Examples of this approach may be found at the Hodgin Elementary School in Albuquerque, New Mexico, and the Evergreen School in Vancouver, Washington. Superior readers in these and other schools are developing creativity through the study of fairytales, fables, and myths. Emphasis is placed on directing or guiding the children in such a manner as to encourage independent action and progress in both reading and creativity. In addition to encouraging free reading and stimulating creativity in oral, written, and artistic expression, these programs seek to develop in the youngsters a new awareness of themselves and their environment. Recordings, films, filmstrips, and various art media are used prior to introducing the children to written materials. Reading is followed by discussion, by creative art activities, and by rewriting and tape recording favorite tales in a modern setting. Small group discussions emphasize discovering motives and feelings of folklore heroes, speculating about how and why folk tales originated, and drawing hypotheses about how the tales might have been altered through the ages as a result of oral transmission. Other creative activities involving dioramas, panel pictures, and pantomime are used to stimulate interest and help make the folk heroes realistic to the beginning reader. Many superior readers obtain more advanced versions of their favorite myths and are able to master the vocabulary independently.

A longstanding program for the gifted in Cleveland, Ohio, has developed a series of enrichment activities in literature for primary youngsters. The program is structured in the form of a literature club, and club activities are divided into a number of "maturity levels" which allow the student to progress individually according to his own rate of comprehension. Although each level focuses on a specific set of basic skills, an equally important objective is that of integrating the basic skills with creative, evaluative, and leadership experience. Each child is encouraged to serve as a group leader in conducting discussions for the literature club. At the conclusion of each session the children evaluate their own progress and the progress of the group. A comprehensive teachers' guide, entitled *A Treasury of Ideas,* includes many helpful hints about conducting club activities and stimulating creative and evaluative thinking.

Special provisions for gifted youngsters in the Cleveland Major Work Classes are also offered beyond the primary level. A detailed description of the "intensive" and "collateral" programing approaches for superior readers has been reported by Barbe and Norris (4). These approaches emphasize the probe for depth of understanding through carefully selected discussion questions and the development of reading tastes through individualized programing that brings the reader into contact with a variety of topics.

In the Wilkes-Barre, Pennsylvania, program extensive and varied reading is engendered by intensive individual research. Pupils are informally taught about the operation of the typewriter and learn ways of typing simple reports. They are encouraged to type their own reports and may use typewriters in most classrooms. Creative writing is a feature of the program as is shown by outstanding poetry, prose, and plays composed by the children.

There are, of course, many youngsters who have been identified as gifted but who experience some difficulty in reading. A number of school districts are making special efforts to help overcome such problems. Intensive instruction in the basic skills through a highly individualized approach is the most frequently reported method for dealing with the reading difficulties of gifted youngsters at the early grade levels.

Representative programs of this type are currently in operation in the public schools of Bellevue, Washington, and Milwaukee, Wisconsin. Careful diagnosis of strengths and weaknesses by a reading specialist is followed by individual prescriptive programing that is developed cooperatively by the reading specialist and the classroom teacher. Remedial activities are selected from a vast assortment of locally developed materials and commercially available skill-building laboratories. Because of the wide range of interests of the gifted child, a diversity of readily available materials is an especially important feature of these programs; and every effort is made to choose a variety of topics that are of particular interest to the individual learner. These topics include stories about animals, mythical heroes, American spacemen, and sports. Another important aspect of this type of program is the charting of each child's achievement. The superior learner tends to progress rapidly in skill development, and the repetitious drill of already mastered skills is avoided because it is likely to lessen the youngster's enthusiasm for reading. By maintaining a weekly and sometimes even daily chart of individual growth, the teachers are able to spot progress readily and adjust each student's program for maximum development and continued interest.

PROGRAMS IN MIDDLE GRADES

Superior readers in the elementary grades usually have mastered the basic skills and literal comprehension; therefore, most of the programs for gifted children at this level tend to emphasize critical comprehension, appreciation of literature, and the development of the ability to read creatively. Although many of the school districts reporting special reading and language arts provisions indicated that the needs of superior students could best be met through individualized reading programs, the districts also pointed out the importance of group work in developing related listening, speaking, and dramatization skills.

The Accelerated Learning Program in Wichita, Kansas, is an example of a comprehensive language arts program that provides a variety of enrichment experiences in the communication skills for able students in grades four, five, and six. Four different reading rates (normal, slow, rapid, and skimming) are developed through the use of materials, such as newspapers, detailed directions, textbooks, advertisements, and books for pleasure. A major goal of the program is to develop critical reading ability through an in-depth analysis of several types of communications media. The children construct lists of criteria for evaluating various materials. Through round-table discussions the children attempt to differentiate facts from opinion; to distinguish changes in feelings, attitudes, and values; to compare different accounts of the same event; to discover the overt and subtle meanings of essays, political cartoons, and editorials; and to analyze material for its emotional appeal, propaganda effect, and writer bias.

Numerous speaking, writing, and independent research activities are used in the Accelerated Learning Classes to promote vocabulary development and creative expression. These activities include holding imaginary telephone conversations with historical persons; writing and telling exaggerated stories and tall tales; building stories from lists of randomly selected characters, events, and places; writing television commercials and setting them to music; constructing lists of similes, metaphors, and picturesque expressions; and writing Haiku and other forms of poetry.

Children's literature, both old and new, is used in the Los Angeles City Schools to explore various types and aspects of literature (6). The students are taught to analyze the motives of fictional characters, to follow plot development, and to interpret mood, theme, and author's purpose. Through an appropriate selection of children's literature, the students gain insight into human behavior and an understanding of environmental influences on character. Various types of poetry also are used to study verse and stanza forms, figurative language, symbolism, theme, and tone.

Two programs for gifted middle-grade youngsters in Connecticut are using the medium of mythology and folklore to explore some of the basic themes in literature, such as the hero concept, predestination, the man-God conflict, and the ancients' use of mythology to explain events in nature. Operation ASTRA in Hartford, Connecticut, and Project CREATE in Bristol, Connecticut, are attempting to promote analytic and comparative abilities by asking youngsters to contrast the personalities, physical characteristics, and accomplishments of real and fictional heroes encountered in literature and in social studies. Through role playing and simulated learning games, the students of mythology are asked to relive the historical events and everyday happenings of ancient times. Emphasis is placed on creating original myths and folktales that might be used to explain natural phenomena, such as the change of seasons and the elephant's long nose. University specialists in mythology and folk literature assist the teachers and students in identifying themes and resource materials around which the studies are built.

A number of middle-grade programs for superior students are focused on developing creative writing and oral communication abilities. Programs emphasizing these objectives were reported by the Grande Prairie School in Albany, Oregon; the Southwest School in Waterford, Connecticut; and the elementary schools in Colorado Springs. Imaginative activities designed to promote divergent thinking have been developed in these and other programs. One of these activities consists in having individual students create detailed character sketches, after which two or three students pool their characters and jointly author short stories and scripts for classroom plays. Another activity deals with creative copywriting, which involves having students write attractive newspaper advertisements for relatively useless objects, such as a broken-down shack on a deserted road in the middle of a swamp. Other activities consist of dramatizing scenes from favorite stories; writing happy, sad, and ridiculous endings to stories in basal readers; developing class newspapers with datelines that coincide with events in history books; and writing historical skits and presenting them to primary grade youngsters. Many activities involve the use of nonverbal creative abilities, such as designing costumes, scenery, and musical accompaniment.

An enrichment program in the Allentown, Pennsylvania, schools includes three levels of Spanish, a correlated creative arts program of art, rhythm and dance, and music. The students also receive special library instruction and opportunities for typing. As a community service, these gifted pupils read and review children's books; some of their reviews have been published in the local press.

Five specific aspects of creative reading that have been identified by DeBoer (7) were found to be operating in varying degrees in a number of elementary programs. The first aspect, creative inquiry, deals with learning how to ask the right questions—questions beyond the informational level that reveal a mature kind of critical curiosity. Creative interpretation involves an intensive effort to reconstruct reading material using the clues and symbols found in the original writing. Creative integration is concerned with combining the words, concepts, and images of a story into a new and sometimes unexpected mood or perception in the reader's mind. The fourth aspect, creative application, involves looking for various situations in the reader's experience that may relate directly or indirectly to what has been read. Finally, creative criticism deals with the process of separating fact from opinion and of drawing tentative conclusions that may be independent of those of the author.

Several schools throughout the country reported making special provisions for their advanced readers in the middle grades through selective use of basal readers, language development kits, reading labs, and the vast assortment of supplementary books and materials that have been developed in recent years. Some of these materials are carefully controlled for level of difficulty and skill development and, therefore, are readily adaptable to the task of matching challenging material with the needs of advanced readers.

PROGRAMS IN JUNIOR HIGH SCHOOL

A variety of imaginative practices was reported for superior readers at the junior high school level. The Ceiling Unlimited project in Brockton, Massachusetts, has developed a unique humanities program built around the central theme of man's understanding of himself. Through extensive independent study and small group discussion, the students explore several aspects of communication and its influence on the development of contemporary culture. The works of Marshall McCluhan, Edward Hall (*The Silent Language*), and other contributors to present-day thought serve as major resources; a comprehensive collection of supplementary books, films, and periodicals that deal with specific aspects of communication are conveniently located in a classroom resource center. Student experimentation in both verbal and nonverbal communication is used to develop proficiency in the methodology of communication research. Ancient and modern foreign languages are studied in addition to English in order to gain a more universal perspective of language usage across time and culture. The culmination of each independent study and experimental investigation involves a student demonstration for the group at large. In presenting their findings, the young researchers select and prepare appropriate media and thereby gain experience in using the many technical facilities available in Ceiling Unlimited. This program also provides the services of a remedial reading specialist for youngsters who are experiencing difficulty in the skills of language development.

At the Maple Heights City Schools in Ohio, an experimental course, Creativity: Concepts and Procedures, is providing opportunities for eighth grade students to become actively engaged in the discovery of creative solutions to environmental problems. The course is offered daily for the entire school year and is coordinated with similar offerings in creativity at the senior high school level. During the early weeks of the course, emphasis is placed on understanding the importance of imagination in problem solving and the analysis of personal and cultural barriers that act as deterrents to creativity. The introductory phase is followed by a study of specific techniques that can be used to overcome the barriers. Such techniques include brainstorming (listing as many ideas as possible within a given period of time without initial concern for the quality of the ideas), attribute listing (examining the purpose and physical characteristics of an object in order to generate ways of improving the object), forced relationships (combining two or more usually unrelated objects and building a story around the forced relationship), and the morphological analysis technique (developing a matrix based on the function and properties of common objects and exploring all possible combinations within the cells of the matrix that might lead to an improved object). Books such as Osborn's *Applied Imagination* (Scribner), Taylor's *How To Create New Ideas* (Prentice-Hall), and Von Fange's *Professional Creativity* (Prentice-Hall), are used as sources to supplement the training process. Following the completion of a unit dealing with problem-solving methods, a highly individualized and flexible format allows students to bring their newly developed strategies to bear on an assortment of problem situations in academic areas, the arts, and the field of human relations. Extensive use is made of closed circuit television; students are given technical assistance in video production through the involvement of personnel from the local television station. Evaluative data gathered at the completion of the project's first year of operation indicate remarkable gains on measures of creativity.

A research center in the humanities is being used at the Mt. Diablo

School District in California to help gifted youngsters develop a personal insight into the value systems of our society. Topics not ordinarily included in the curriculum are pursued on both a group and individual basis during the academic year and in a special summer session. These topics include religion and philosophy, opera, ballet, theater, photography, and other humanistic studies. Special activities—such as, hypothetical United Nations sessions, man-on-the-street interviews, and original plays and stories depicting cultural conflicts—are used to pursue the general "way of life" theme which guides the project. Extensive use is made of the human and community resources of the region.

The Columbia View School in Portland, Oregon, uses the medium of motion pictures to develop a greater appreciation of literary technique on the part of gifted junior high school students. A literature teacher, a school librarian, and a specialist in instructional materials work as a team in developing and implementing a series of activities that deal with aspects of literature, such as metaphor, simile, symbolism, and characterization. The students apply their skills in these areas by producing original films and videotaping programs.

A number of programs at the junior high school level focus on the development of creative writing abilities. The Young Authors Project carried out at the reading center in Evansville, Indiana; the creative writing workshops in the San Diego City Schools; and the Major Work classes in Cleveland attempt to foster verbal creativity. In the San Diego program, enthusiasm is generated by involving professional writers from the community who work closely with individual students and assist in conducting the workshops. Outstanding poems, stories, and essays are combined with creative works in the graphic arts to produce an annual student publication entitled *Quests*.

A popular approach at the junior high school level is the use of the Junior Great Books Program. Critical reading and thinking are the major objectives of this highly developed system which emphasizes an in-depth probing for meaning through the use of carefully formulated discussion questions. The philosophy behind this program is that each learner comes to grips with the material in a way that is significant for him in terms of his own background, capacity, attitude, and interest. The Great Books Foundation has developed a series of materials that can be used with students from the third grade through the senior high school. The following schools reported using all or part of the Junior Great Books Programs: the Yankee Ridge School in Urbana, Illinois; the Demonstration Centers for Gifted in Charleston and Flossmoor, Illinois; the William Byrne Elementary

School in Burnsville, Minnesota; the Cupertino School District in California; and the Wheat Ridge Junior High School in Jefferson County, Colorado.

PROGRAMS IN SENIOR HIGH SCHOOL

Programs for superior students at the senior high school level generally focus on enrichment experiences in literature and humanities. At the Twin Cities Institute for Talented Youth in Minneapolis-St. Paul, a summer program that serves students from more than fifty high schools is using a team teaching approach to pursue a variety of studies in the humanities as well as in other areas. The curricular content deals mainly with topics which are highly relevant for today's youth. Contemporary poetry and theater, film making, modern rhetoric, and black literature are a few of the studies offered by the institute. Through individual and small group instruction, the students have an opportunity to work closely with authorities from various fields and to participate actively in projects which use the entire city as a learning environment.

A number of high schools across the nation have developed interesting approaches to the humanities. At the Effingham High School in Illinois, a senior rhetoric class is using an inductive approach and purposeful daily composition activity to promote efficient and economical patterns of thinking and writing. The Stevens High School in Claremont, New Hampshire, combines history, art, architecture, literature, and music in studying the ages of man from the time of the Greeks to the twentieth century. A similar approach is used in the high schools of Boise, Idaho, where a central theme of "Man's Search for Identity" is employed as the core around which a course in the humanities is structured. A program at the senior high school in Langley, Washington, uses an extensive collection of records, tapes, and slides to integrate music and art into the study of classic and modern literature.

Although most of the school districts responding to the survey indicated that literature and the humanities were primary concerns at the senior high school level, a number of schools reported programs which emphasize study habits and developmental reading. In Beverly Hills, California, academically talented students in grades nine through twelve participate in a seminar program which is conducted under the leadership of a student director (8). The reading and study skills consultant serves as a resource person and assists in identifying topics and skills that will promote good reading habits and learning skills. In West Palm Beach, Florida, a reading skills laboratory in the high school enables gifted students to improve their reading rates on an individual basis. Courses in developmental reading at Keene High School in New Hampshire and at Westwood High School in Mesa, Arizona, are designed to increase general reading ability for college-bound students. Emphasis is placed on reading in various content areas, comprehension, study skills, and acquiring a flexible speed reading rate. Diagnostic testing and individual counseling enable each student to determine his needs and to plan a program that is uniquely suited to his interests and purpose.

SUMMARY

In this chapter, representative innovative practices that are currently being used to improve opportunities for gifted students are described. Attention is directed to practices which focus on reading and the language arts.

In reading, the use of various media and supplementary reading materials suggests a tendency to depart from the influence of basal reading texts. The frequent appearance of individualized reading programs at all levels suggests a growing awareness that the gifted student has unique reading needs that cannot be dealt with adequately in highly structured group situations through limited reading materials. Today the reading teacher frequently has at his disposal a wide selection of trade books, reading laboratories, and instructional aids; these materials are increasingly employed to assist in planning for the gifted and creative pupil in ways that challenge his abilities and foster his interest in reading.

There is also an encouraging tendency to broaden the objectives of reading instruction. More and more, a broad criterion of reading is being used. Moreover, programs are increasingly being devised to promote the use of higher mental processes and are being associated more often with creative expression in the language arts.

REFERENCES

1. Barbe, Walter B. "A Study of Reading of Gifted High School Students," *Educational Administration and Supervision,* 21 (December 1954), 84-87.
2. Barbe, Walter B. "Problems in Reading Encountered by Gifted," *Elementary English,* 33 (May 1956), 274-278.
3. Barbe, Walter B. "Reading Aspects," in L. A. Fliegler (Ed.), *Curriculum Planning for the Gifted.* Englewood Cliffs, New Jersey: Prentice-Hall, 1961, 214-243.
4. Barbe, Walter B., and Dorothy E. Norris. "Reading Instruction in Special Classes for Elementary Gifted Children," *Reading Teacher,* 16 (May 1963), 425-428.

5. Bigaj, James J. "A Reading Program for Gifted Children in the Primary Grades," in J. Allen Figurel (Ed.), *Reading and Realism,* 1968 Proceedings, Volume 13, Part 1. Newark, Delaware: International Reading Association, 1969, 144-148.

6. Black, Millard H. "A Reading Program for Gifted Children in the Middle Grades," in J. Allen Figurel (Ed.), *Reading and Realism,* 1968 Proceedings, Volume 13, Part 1. Newark, Delaware: International Reading Association, 1969, 148-150.

7. DeBoer, John J. "Creative Reading and the Gifted Student," *Reading Teacher,* 16 (May 1963), 435-441.

8. Sparks, J. E. "Experience Needs of Capable Students," in J. Allen Figurel (Ed.), *Reading and Inquiry,* 1965 Proceedings of the International Reading Association, 10. Newark, Delaware: International Reading Association, 1965, 57-59.

9. Strang, Ruth. "Gifted Children Need Help in Reading, Too," *Reading Teacher,* 6 (January 1953), 23.

10. Strang, Ruth. "Psychology of Gifted Children and Youth," in William Cruickshank (Ed.), *Psychology of Exceptional Children and Youth.* Englewood Cliffs, New Jersey: Prentice-Hall, 1955, 489-490.

11. Terman, Lewis, and Melita Oden. *Genetic Studies of Genius,* Volumes I-V. Stanford, California: Stanford University Press, 1925-1959.

12. Tisdall, William J. "Meeting the Reading Needs of the Mentally Advanced," paper presented at the Twentieth Annual Conference and Course in Reading, University of Pittsburgh, July 10, 1964, 10, 16-20. (Reprint)

13. Witty, Paul, and H. C. Lehman. "A Study of the Reading and Reading Interests of Gifted Children," *Journal of Genetic Psychology,* 40 (June 1932), 473-485.

14. Witty, Paul (Ed.) *Development in and through Reading,* National Society for the Study of Education Yearbook, Part I. Chicago: University of Chicago, 1961, 1.

15. Witty, Paul. "Enriching the Reading of the Gifted Child," *Library Journal,* 20 (November 15, 1955), 2622.

16. Witty, Paul. "Reading for the Gifted," in J. Allen Figurel (Ed.), *Reading and Realism,* 1968 Proceedings, Volume 13, Part 1. Newark, Delaware: International Reading Association, 1969, 47-55.

17. Witty, Paul. *Reading in Modern Education.* Boston: D.C. Heath, 1949.

18. Witty, Paul et al. *The Teaching of Reading—A Developmental Process.* Boston: D.C. Heath, 1966.

CHAPTER 4

The Role of the Parent of Gifted and Creative Children

Edith H. Grotberg

THE IMPORTANCE of the role of the parents is often underestimated in the preschool educational program. Schools tend to discourage parental involvement in the formal learning experiences of young children. This restriction is frequently the result of the belief that parents, because they lack professional training, are inadequate as teachers. It is also the result of the belief that development is genetically determined and not influenced greatly by environmental factors. Therefore, little intellectual stimulation is given the child before he enters school. Witty (*18*) summarized the view as follows:

> There has, unfortunately, been a great neglect of intellectual stimulation for young children at home. This condition has persisted in many kindergartens and first grades. One reason is to be found in the long prevailing conviction among educators that intelligence, especially as shown by IQ, is largely unaffected by environmental factors.
>
> For many years the IQ was regarded as being chiefly an expression of an inborn capacity which developed according to a fixed rate.

The concept of genetic determinism continues to dominate the thinking of some parents even after the child enters school. Many parents, like many teachers, seem to believe that intelligence is inborn; hence it is desirable to postpone instruction until children have matured sufficiently to profit from such reading instruction. Some believe that the "right time" for reading instruction is when the child has attained perhaps a mental age above six or six and one-half years. Thus, their attitudes are similar to those of many

33

educators who also doubt the possibility that early stimulation and wide opportunities for learning will affect learning ability greatly. School personnel sometimes question also the typical parent's capability of offering effective instruction in reading.

Parents of gifted youngsters are often greatly influenced by the attitudes of teachers and administrators concerning their participation in the education of children. They may have a three- or four-year-old child who persists in asking questions about letters, words, and books. On consulting teachers at school about what to do with their inquisitive, impatient child, parents may be led to feel guilty of trying to exploit him. Teachers sometimes warn such parents about possible emotional harm that may result from pressures to force children to learn before they are ready. These parents may return home discouraged and disarmed. This outcome is unfortunate since such parents usually want only to do what is best for their children. Rather than run the risk of harming their children, they may abandon efforts to provide intellectual nurture at home and may redirect their children's activities into less controversial pursuits.

Such procedures and attitudes are out of harmony with the facts recently disclosed by cognitive psychologists who stress the potentiality of children for successful and beneficial learning during the early years. It is now clearly established that parents may play a critical role in stimulating the wholesome development of gifted and creative children before they enter school, as well as during the school years. Moreover, parents may impede development by failure to provide rich and varied intellectual stimulation for young children.

Investigators stress the fact that deprivation of experiences may be a powerful force in determining the lack of "readiness" of disadvantaged children for successful school work. It has been shown that such children have vast and undeveloped potentialities for successful learning.

The acquisitions of children during the early years are, of course, influenced greatly by cultural and ethnic factors. Thus, Stodolsky and Lesser (*15*) examined four mental abilities (verbal ability, reasoning, number facility, and space conceptualization) in four ethnic groups (Chinese, Jewish, Negro, and Puerto Rican) with each ethnic group divided into middle- and lower-class children. They found that ethnic group membership has a marked effect on the pattern of performance. The Chinese group, for example, encouraged the development of spatial skills, and their children performed in a superior way on tests involving spatial relations. In contrast, the Jewish group stressed verbal skills and placed little emphasis on spatial skills. The Jewish children succeeded in making the highest verbal scores among the ethnic groups studied. This finding is in accord with other investigations. Thus, Barbe (2) reported that "the Jewish group appears to be represented in far greater numbers (among the gifted) than its proportional share."

The socioeconomic level of the family is also related to the intellectual expression of children. Thus, many low-income families, preoccupied with meeting needs for food, clothing, and shelter, neglect to provide the experiences, stimulation, and encouragement necessary for the maximum intellectual development of their young children. Middle-class children, on the other hand, usually have a greater stimulation and opportunity to acquire the language skills and other requirements of formal education and, as a result, score higher in reading and linguistic tests and succeed better in school.

Family interests and activities are also related to children's achievement. Thus, it was found that middle-class parents of children in a nursery school traveled more and had a larger number of hobbies than the low-income parents. In addition, they took their children more frequently to visit the library, the post office, zoos, museums, and department stores and provided more often materials such as books, pencils, and crayons at home. Hence, it is not surprising that gifted children were identified more frequently in middle-class families than in lower-income groups. Parents of gifted children should, therefore, recognize the varied factors that are associated with giftedness in children. Gifted children are more likely to be found in ethnic or racial groups that are able to offer young children rich and diversified experiences and varied opportunities for learning. They are also more likely to be found in homes of superior socioeconomic status wherein learning experiences tend to be richer and more varied than in the homes of less fortunate parents of lower socioeconomic status. Thus, it appears that a rich environmental background may strongly influence the development of the abilities measured by intelligence tests which reflect not only hereditary factors but also environmental influences.

There are certain characteristics of young gifted children that parents should recognize. These characteristics should guide them in their search for signs of giftedness in children. After many years of study of this topic, Witty (*19*) concluded:

> These studies make it possible to set forth, with considerable clarity, the characteristics of such children. These studies suggest the importance to the child's later development of early identification and of parent understanding of his nature and needs.
>
> Evidence of superiority may be readily observed in most gifted children when they are very young. Some of the characteristics of such children follow:

1. The early use of a large vocabulary, accurately employed.
2. Language proficiency—the use of phrases and entire sentences at a very early age, and the ability to tell or reproduce a story at an early age.
3. Keen observation and retention of information about things observed.
4. Interest in or liking for books—later enjoyment of atlases, dictionaries, and encyclopedia.
5. Early interest in calendars and in clocks.
6. The ability to attend or concentrate for a longer period than is typical of most children.
7. Demonstrations of proficiency in drawing, music, and other art forms.
8. Early discovery of cause-and-effect relationships.
9. The early development of ability to read.
10. The development of varied interests.

The preceding list should be helpful to parents as they attempt to appraise their children's abilities impartially. Parents must be zealous not to overestimate or to underestimate a child's ability. They should accept his gifts gladly and provide him with the recognition and encouragement that his abilities warrant. Of course, parents should learn about the development of typical children as well as of gifted children in order to make accurate judgments.

PARENTS AND HOMES OF THE GIFTED AND CREATIVE

It has long been recognized that gifted and creative children come from homes that provide special opportunities for learning and frequent encouragement. Thus, one investigator (*18*) summarized the findings of research on the gifted and their homes in this way:

> The characteristics of superior home environments have been repeatedly shown. . . . For example, the gifted children studied by the writer came from homes of superior socioeconomic status. In these homes, abundant opportunities were given for varied experience and for exploration of the environment. Sensory-motor activities were usually rich and varied, as were language experiences. Many other opportunities for wholesome activity and intellectual stimulation were found in these homes. Moreover, the parents usually recognized the superior ability of their children and encouraged its expression and development.

Some parents of gifted children encourage early learning in their children and provide varied opportunities for development. Others, however, provide a meager background and withhold encouragement of varied learning experiences. One result of such deprivation is underachievement in school. The homes of gifted underachievers are beset with problems which consume the attention and energies of the parents and often are permeated by tension and conflict. Gowan (7) points to some of the problems gifted underachievers experience in their homes:

1. Disagreement between the parents, and of the parents with their parents, over methods of rearing the child.
2. Transference of problems of parents to the child.
3. Overanxiety or overprotectiveness on the part of the parent.
4. Fears of parents regarding the child's health or safety.
5. Divorces or separations of parents.
6. Parent's failure to prepare child for the birth of a new baby.

A pattern of parental indifference, rejection, or oversolicitude is reported repeatedly in other studies (8, 14). The relationship between the attitudes of parents and children's behavior is critical in the development and expression of gifts in children. Support and motivation offered in early childhood foster self-confidence and the resultant expression of talents.

EARLY IDENTIFICATION AND MOTIVATION

Recent studies lead one to question some widely held views about gifted children. For example, it is untenable to assert "that intellectual precocity is somehow not quite healthy, is almost always a hazard to good social adjustment, and should be slowed down rather than facilitated" (13). Pressey examined the home background and early childhood experiences of outstanding adults who were considered "precocious musicians and athletes." He found that the promise of most of these remarkable people was recognized at a very young age. Furthermore, they were consistently encouraged by their parents and other adults around them. Pressey (13) analyzed the factors that recurred as correlates to outstanding attainment and concluded:

1. Precocious musicians and athletes usually had excellent early opportunities for the ability to develop and encouragement from family and friends.
2. Usually individuals who developed precocious excellence had superior early and continuing individual guidance and instruction.
3. Precocious individuals have had the opportunity frequently and continuingly to practice and extend their special ability and to progress as they were able.
4. The special precocious ability usually brought a close association with

others in the field, which greatly fostered the abilities of all concerned, and led to a still wider stimulating acquaintance.

5. As a result of many opportunities for real accomplishment, within his possibilities but of increasing challenge, the precocious musician or athlete has had the stimulation of many and increasingly strong success experiences—and his world acclaimed these successes.

Thus, early recognition and praise for success are shown to be strong influences in fostering the development of gifts and talents. Witty (*18*) underscores the foregoing conclusions in his descriptions of gifted children. Many of these children learned to read before entering school in homes in which the environment was rich in the essentials of early learning. The parents frequently fostered reading by encouraging firsthand experience, by reading aloud to their children, by answering their questions directly and patiently, and by providing a varied assortment of children's magazines, picture books, and other resources. Moreover, they showed their own respect for and enjoyment of reading by their own wide reading. Frequently, the services of the public library were added to the resources of the home. These environmental conditions are described more fully in Chapter 2 of this monograph.

Such environmental conditions undoubtedly played an important role in accelerating the learning ability and may have led to an increase in the intelligence ratings of the group.

IMPORTANCE OF EARLY LEARNING

Comparisons of the environment of impoverished children with that of the gifted described previously reinforce the conclusion that opportunities for early learning are crucial if children are to realize their potentialities. Thus, Bloom, Davis, and Hess (*5*) emphasize the importance of a rich environment for perceptual development:

Perceptual development is stimulated by environments which are rich in the range of experiences available; which make use of games, toys, and many objects for manipulation; and in which there is frequent interaction between the child and adults at meals, playtimes, and throughout the day. At the beginning of the first grade there are differences between culturally deprived and culturally advantaged children in the amount and variety of experiences they have had in their perceptual development.

Bloom (*4*) emphasizes the importance of opportunities for early diversified experiences and learning for three reasons:

The first is based on the very rapid growth of selected characteristics in the early years and conceives of the variations in the early environment as so important because they shape these characteristics in their most rapid periods of formation.

Another way of viewing the importance of the early environment has to do with the sequential nature of much of human development. Each characteristic is built on a base of that same characteristic at an earlier time or on the base of other characteristics which precede it in development.

A third reason for the crucial importance of the early environment and early experiences stems from learning theory. . . . Although each learning theory may explain the phenomenon in different ways, most would agree that the first learning takes place more easily than a later one that is interfered with by an earlier learning.

It has been shown, too, that lack of varied early learning experiences may impede development and have far-reaching adverse effects.

PARENTS CAN HELP

With the foregoing facts about early learning in mind, parents may inquire: What can we do to foster learning and promote the development of gifts and talents in our gifted children before they enter school? And what is the parent's responsibility to the gifted child during the school years?

The following suggestions are offered:

1. Parents should recognize themselves as teachers. They teach by example, by providing materials for learning, by approving or disapproving their children's behavior, by interacting with their children, and by patient guidance. In other words, parents should use many of the techniques of good teachers. The difference is that parents often do not realize that they *are* teachers and are unaware of the kinds of learning they may foster or neglect. As they become appreciative of their role as teachers, they may become more successful in fostering learning in their children.

2. Parents should interact with their children verbally, intellectually, socially, and emotionally. This conduct is particularly important for gifted children. The verbally gifted child, for example, needs to hear the many ways words are used as well as to have the opportunity to use new words or to use words in new contexts. Gifted and creative children need to think with their parents in discussions as they learn how to reason and to communicate effectively. Parents of the gifted should find time for these important relationships with their children. The parents' role in the age of TV is increasingly complex. Witty has shown in yearly studies of televiewing

by parents, children, and teachers, started in 1949 and continued to the present, the way TV consumes the lion's share of the leisure time of children and young people. He has suggested procedures parents and teachers may employ in studying the influence of the mass media and has suggested ways of relating this strong interest to varied reading experiences. He concludes (*17*) as follows:

> We have briefly indicated some of the research studies made during the past decade and a half which reveal facts about the nature and extent of children's televiewing. And we have cited also research concerning the effects of TV on boys and girls. The research is meager and needs to be extended by far more comprehensive and ingenious efforts. There is a great need for more widespread attempts to offer effective guidance and supervision both in school and at home.
>
> At present there are many mediocre TV programs and far too many offerings which feature violence. But there are also programs, both commercial and educational, which are desirable for children. And there are occasional presentations of rare beauty and high merit which boys and girls should see. Children should be led to choose such programs voluntarily and to discriminate in their selections generally. We should take advantage of children's interest in TV. Research students should direct attention to discovering ways to obtain greater benefits from the universal appeal of the electronic Pied Piper.

3. Parents should show that they are dependable, reliable persons whom children can admire and emulate. Children's learning is impaired when parents ignore them, mislead them, or are inconsistent in their behavior toward them. Children need to trust their parents as teachers since early learning is accepted on faith in the person who instructs them. When children lose this faith or trust, their learning is adversely affected. Patience and understanding are needed on the part of parents.

4. Parents should encourage rich and varied first-hand experiences in their children. Sensorimotor activities should be introduced early and adapted to each child's ability and needs. It is true, of course, that such experiences are frequently found in the homes of gifted children. However, there are many homes that do not afford opportunities of these kinds. In these homes, suggestions that appear in the guide for the *Adventures in Discovery* program may be followed advantageously. Suggestions are also found in the SRA booklet *Helping the Gifted Child*. One of the most useful books for parents of the gifted is Beck's perceptive volume *How to Raise a Brighter Child* (*3*).

5. Parents should encourage language expression and should try to answer gifted children's questions in terms that are readily understood. In

Witty's studies, age four appeared to be the golden age for questions. At this time, parents are the child's most influential teachers. They need insight and wise discrimination in their efforts to help their children. Again, the suggestions of Beck are especially useful.

6. Parents should listen to children as they tell their stories and should be prepared to tell stories to children. Some parents of gifted children have become expert in the art of storytelling.

7. Parents should provide an assortment of picture books for discussion and enjoyment. They should also read aloud varied materials and should have available an assortment of children's literature including children's magazines, such as *Highlights for Children*.

8. When a child requests help in printing and saying words, he should be given assistance. Young gifted children will often succeed in printing words, sentences, and even short stories. They will sometimes request help in spelling and will enjoy sounding out the letters of the alphabet. Help should be given at this time to children. It should not be delayed until the child enters school when it is too late for most advantageous use. Pertinent suggestions are found in *Helping the Gifted Child*.

We have already pointed out that many gifted children learn to read before they enter school. They have frequently had the advantage of diversified learning activities in homes of sympathetic and resourceful parents who try to provide appropriate conditions and opportunities for their children's development during the early years. As the writer has already indicated, these varied activities include the encouragement of language expression and the provision of books and other printed materials to extend experience, satisfy interests, and engender joy in reading.

Exercises, activities, and materials which foster early learning in gifted as well as other children are described in greater detail in a number of books and magazines which are listed here. Parents may be aided by examining the following sources.

MATERIALS ON CHILD DEVELOPMENT

Anderson, Vera Dieckman. *Reading and Young Children*. New York: Macmillan 1968, 58-126.
Written especially for parents and teachers of young children.

Beck, Joan. *How to Raise a Brighter Child*. New York: Trident Press, 1967.
Written for parents; discusses ways to provide a variety of intellectually stimulating experiences for children; is practical, provocative, and inspiring.

Bloom, Benjamin S. *Stability and Change in Human Characteristics*. New York: John Wiley and Sons, 1964.

Recommended for the parent who wishes to examine scientific studies.

Engleman, Siegfried, and Therese Englemann. *Give Your Child a Superior Mind*. New York: Simon and Schuster, 1961.

Outlines a program for parents and suggests a variety of word and number games which parents may use.

Golden First Adventures in Learning Program. Revised in 1970 as *Adventures in Discovery*. New York: Western Publishing Company.

Prepared for children ages three to five.

Highlights for Children, Highlights for Teachers, and related *Handbooks*. Columbus, Ohio: Highlights for Children.

Contains materials of value for inspiring learning in young children.

Hunt, J. McV. *Intelligence and Experience*. New York: Ronald Press, 1961.

Deals with insight derived from investigations by scholars.

Jenkins, Gladys G., and others. *These Are Your Children*. Chicago: Scott, Foresman, 1949.

Recommended as a valuable volume about children and their growth.

Kirk, S.A. *Early Education of the Mentally Retarded*. Urbana, Illinois: University of Illinois Press, 1958.

Presents provocative suggestions for parents of exceptional children.

Pines, Maya. *Revolution in Learning—The Years from Birth to Six*. New York: Harper and Row, 1966.

Provides a readable and helpful account of change in attitudes.

Witty, Paul A., and Edith H. Grotberg. *Helping the Gifted Child* (Rev. ed.). Chicago: Science Research Associates, 1970.

Makes helpful suggestions for aiding the gifted.

Studies of the gifted consistently show that almost half learned to read before entering school. Most of those who learned to read did so not entirely alone. Usually members of the family had read to them and had taken time to answer questions. Parents, then, can help preschool children learn to read on an informal basis by providing books, by reading to the children, and by thoughtfully answering questions.

The parents' task is not completed when the child enters school. The parents' role continues to be significant as he cooperates with teachers in guiding and promoting developmental reading.

Parents should work closely with teachers to assure conditions in school that promote a balanced and individually appropriate program of reading for each child. It is especially desirable that the gifted child's remarkable ability be recognized at every level in his education and that he be offered materials of suitable difficulty to challenge his ability and foster his development. The gifted child requires guidance in accord with his unique nature and needs. He also needs a program that is geared to his interests. During adolescence, many gifted youths will meet problems in personal and social adjustment. Reading may prove to be a great help in meeting such problems.

Teachers, librarians, and parents should strive to pool their resources to help gifted pupils and young people to realize the inexhaustible wealth of information and pleasure to be derived from good books.

There are a number of books about reading that are addressed to parents. The following list is perhaps representative and may prove to be of value.

MATERIALS ABOUT READING FOR PARENTS

Adventuring with Books. Elizabeth Guilfoile and others. A Signet Book, 1966.

> Offers a comprehensive guide to 1,250 books for children, ages three to fourteen.

Arbuthnot, May Hill. *Children's Reading in the Home.* Chicago: Scott, Foresman, 1969.

> Contains an annotated bibliography of stories, poems, and drama organized according to special interest categories.

Carlson, G. R. *Books and the Teenage Reader.* New York: Harper and Row, 1967.

> Contains lists of various types of appealing books.

Frank, Josette. *Your Child's Reading Today* (rev. ed.). Garden City, New York: Doubleday, 1969.

> Evaluates reading activities and books and makes recommendations to parents.

Gagliardo, Ruth. Articles concerning children's literature. Chicago: *The PTA Magazine.*

Larrick, Nancy. *A Parent's Guide to Children's Reading* (3rd rev. ed.). Garden City, New York: Doubleday, 1969.

> Offers annotated bibliography of books organized according to interest areas. An inspiring volume for parents.

Let's Read Together—Books for Family Enjoyment (3rd ed.). Chicago: American Library Association, 1969.

> Lists books selected and annotated by a special committee.

Prescott, Orville. *A Father Reads to His Children.* New York: E.P. Dutton, 1965.

> Contains an excellent collection of twenty-four stories and twenty-four poems chosen for fathers to read aloud to their children.

Willard, C. B., and Helen I. Stapp. *Your Reading.* Champaign, Illinois: National Council of Teachers of English, 1966.

> Suggests books for junior and senior high school students.

Witty, Paul A. "Reading for the Gifted," in J. Allen Figurel (Ed.), *Reading and Realism,* 1968 Proceedings, Volume 13, Part 1. Newark, Delaware:

International Reading Association, 1969, 47-55.
    Offers suggestions for an effective reading program.
Witty, Paul A. "Some Research on TV," in *Children and TV—Television's Impact on the Child*. Washington, D.C.: Association for Childhood Education International, 1967, 15-20.
    Discusses research and studies of televiewing, 1949-1967.

Summary and Conclusions

Information from studies directly focusing on the gifted and creative as well as from studies of the effects of human deprivation makes clear the importance of the early years in the development of exceptional individuals. An examination of the homes of both the gifted and the deprived suggests further the significance of both cultural tradition and socioeconomic levels as they enhance or restrict intellectual performance.

The need for early recognition of gifted and creative children and the importance of consistent and continuous motivation of their learning are stressed. Ways of offering effective help are also indicated. It is pointed out that parents may become effective teachers of the young child. Bibliographies of books related to both early learning and to reading activities are included.

There is evidence that parents play a critical role in the lives of gifted and creative children throughout their development. Greatly needed is attention on the part of parents to the encouragement of their children's reading throughout the elementary and the secondary school. Parents should cooperate closely with teachers and librarians in furthering and extending reading interests and in fostering the ability of children and young people to read critically, creatively, and with enjoyment.

References

1. Barbe, Walter B. "Identification of Gifted Children," *Education*, 88 (September-October 1967), 11-14.
2. Barbe, Walter B. "A Study of the Family Background of the Gifted," *Journal of Educational Psychology*, 47 (May 1956), 302-309.
3. Beck, Joan. *How to Raise a Brighter Child*. New York: Trident Press, 1967.
4. Bloom, Benjamin S. *Stability and Change in Human Characteristics*. New York: John Wiley and Sons, 1964, 214-216.
5. Bloom, Benjamin S., Allison Davis, and Robert Hess. *Compensatory Education for Cultural Deprivation*. New York: Holt, Rinehart and Winston, 1965, 13.

6. Eckland, Bruce, and Donald P. Kent. "Socialization and Social Structure," *Perspectives on Human Deprivation: Biological, Psychological, and Sociological,* NICHD, Public Health Service, U.S. Department of Health, Education and Welfare, 1968, 185-228.

7. Gowan, John C. "The Underachieving Gifted Child, A Problem for Everyone," *Exceptional Children,* 21 (April 1955), 247-249.

8. Grotberg, Edith H. "Adjustment Problems of the Gifted," *Education,* 82 (April 1962), 472-476.

9. Grotberg, Edith H. "Learning Disabilities and Remediation in Disadvantaged Children," *Review of Educational Research,* 35 (December 1965), 413-425.

10. Grotberg, Edith H. (Ed.) *Critical Issues in Research Related to Disadvantaged Children.* Princeton, New Jersey: Educational Testing Service, 1969.

11. Grotberg, Edith H. *Review of Research: 1965-1969—Project Head Start,* Office of Economic Opportunity Pamphlet 6108-13, 1969.

12. Lindsley, Donald, and Austin Riesen. "Biological Substrates of Development and Behavior," *Perspectives on Human Deprivation: Biological, Psychological, and Sociological,* NICHD, Public Health Service, U.S. Department of Health, Education and Welfare, 1968, 229-269.

13. Pressey, Sidney L. "Concerning the Nature and Nurture of Genius," *Scientific Monthly,* 81 (September 1955), 123-129.

14. Roesslein, Charles G. *Differential Patterns of Intelligence Traits between High Achieving and Low Achieving High School Boys.* Washington, D.C.: Catholic University of America Press, 1953.

15. Stodolsky, Susan S., and Gerald Lesser. "Learning Patterns in the Disadvantaged," *Harvard Educational Review,* 37 (Fall 1967), 546-593.

16. Witty, Paul A. "Reading for the Gifted," in J. Allen Figurel (Ed.), *Reading and Realism,* 1968 Proceedings, Volume 13, Part 1. Newark, Delaware: International Reading Association, 1969, 47-55.

17. Witty, Paul A. "Some Research on TV," *Children and TV—Television's Impact on the Child.* Washington, D.C.: Association for Childhood Education International, 1967, 15-20.

18. Witty, Paul A. "Studies of Early Learning—Their Nature and Significance," *Education,* 89 (September-October), 1968, 4-10.

19. Witty, Paul A. "Who Are the Gifted?" in Nelson B. Henry (Ed.), *Education for the Gifted,* Fifty-seventh Yearbook of the National Society for the Study of Education. Chicago: University of Chicago Press, 1958, 48-49.

20. Witty, Paul A., and Mary Ellen Batinich. "A 1967 Study of Televiewing," in J. Allen Figurel (Ed.), *Reading and Realism,* 1968 Proceedings, Volume 13, Part 1. Newark, Delaware: International Reading Association, 1969, 732-735.

CHAPTER 5

The Role of the Teacher of Gifted and Creative Children

Joan B. Nelson and Donald L. Cleland

IN ALL EDUCATIONAL programs, the teacher is the key to effective learning. This fact has been shown repeatedly in studies of the value of various methods of teaching reading to primary grade children (6). In Chapter 2 of this monograph, studies are discussed which make it clear that the way the teacher proceeds is more important than the materials or the specific methods utilized. It is the teacher who sets the environment which inspires or destroys self-confidence, encourages or suppresses interests, develops or neglects abilities, fosters or banishes creativity, stimulates or discourages critical thinking, and facilitates or frustrates achievement.

Implicit in the consideration of the role of the teacher of gifted and creative children is the assumption that this role differs in some substantive way from the role of the teacher in general. Are there specific traits which characterize the successful teacher of the gifted? Does the role require deviance in intellectual aptitude and creativity similar to gifted children themselves? Are there knowledges, understandings, methods, techniques, and materials which are unique to effective teaching of the gifted?

There has been little research indicating characteristics that identify successful teachers of the gifted. Indeed, there is little research to indicate those traits which differentiate between good and poor teachers in general. The attributes most frequently cited as appropriate for teachers of the gifted are the same attributes as those desirable for any good teacher. Lists of desirable traits usually include good health and stamina, knowledge of content field, broad background of information in related fields, a knowledge of the psychology of learning, familiarity with varied teaching methods, patience, creativity, flexibility, and a supportive attitude. Case studies have suggested rather clearly the importance of the teacher's ability to employ child-study techniques to determine the nature and needs of gifted children. Studies have revealed also the value of proficiency on the part of the teacher in using children's literature to satisfy interests and needs (8). Surely, the teacher of gifted children should possess the aforementioned characteristics and should be acquainted with the particular needs and interests of the gifted (7, 8).

The special problems associated with the teaching of the gifted are often basically the problems of dealing with individual differences in children (3, 4). The apparent differences in teaching roles may be based upon the unique characteristics that the gifted child brings to the learning situation and the way that the teacher reacts and responds to these characteristics. If one subscribes to the philosophy of education which recognizes individual differences and seeks to develop each child's unique capabilities and talents to that child's full potential, there can be no doubt that teacher's roles must vary according to the attributes of the students they teach.

What are the implications of this philosophy for the teacher of gifted children? What should be the components of a reading program for the gifted?

IMPLICATIONS FOR THE TEACHER

The teacher must possess an understanding of self. The learning of children is influenced not only by what teachers do but also by what they are. It would be foolish to assume that a person can understand the needs, feelings, and behaviors of others if he does not understand himself. In dealing with students, the good teacher is constantly evaluating his own feelings, perceptions, motivations, and abilities.

Even the decision to work with gifted children must be based on the teacher's awareness of his own strengths and limitations. Gifted children progress most satisfactorily under teachers of superior intelligence who have a broad, general knowledge as well as a thorough mastery of subject area. To meet the demands put upon them, teachers must know subjects and their sources. It is very difficult to "fake it" with gifted students. Their superior reasoning ability and questioning attitude are apt to cause the faker some very uncomfortable moments. A simple, "I don't know; let's find out," creates greater respect and trust between student and teacher than any attempt to deceive. A persistent gap, however, between student need for information and guidance and teacher ability to present or direct students to significant data can be discouraging. Only the teacher who knows his limitations can make an intelligent assessment of his ability to work with the gifted.

Teachers must also examine their feelings about gifted children. The inquisitiveness and questioning attitude typical of gifted children can be a constant source of irritation for an authoritarian teacher. Explanations which are accepted by most children may be questioned or rejected by gifted children. If a teacher shows resentment at a challenging question, he may destroy incipient curiosity. The teacher who is open to new ideas and experiences expands the dimensions of student interests.

The teacher must possess an understanding of giftedness. Giftedness has been defined in various ways (2, 3). Some educators define it in terms of intellectual capacity; others, as consistently outstanding performance in one or more areas of endeavor. Some educators believe that the gifted child may be identified by a constellation of factors which includes intelligence, creativity, drive, perseverance, and performance.

It is extremely important that the verbally gifted child's ability be recognized early in his school career to insure a learning program that challenges him. Though we rarely hear of gifted children failing in school work, many do fail to develop more than a small measure of their potential for learning because of pressure to conformity in undifferentiated programs. Since it is the teacher who comes in personal contact with all the children, it is he who is most likely to identify the gifted children in his charge. For this reason it is vital that every teacher know the characteristics of gifted children.

Although there is no entirely adequate composite of traits for the gifted child, there are several compilations which provide a basis for the teacher in the identification of gifted children (7, 8). These characteristics are set forth in Chapters 2 and 5 of this monograph. Included are the following items which apply primarily to the verbally gifted:

- Better health, social adjustment, and physical endowment
- Longer attention span
- Larger vocabulary
- Greater fluency of ideas
- Greater intellectual curiosity
- More rapid and efficient learning
- Greater ability to generalize and form concepts
- Greater insight into problems

- More curiosity and interest in intellectual tasks
- Earlier reading attainment (sometimes before school entrance)
- Wider range of interests

Teachers should be aware also of certain traits and behaviors which characterize highly creative children:

- Less concern with convention and authority
- More independence in judgment and thinking
- Keener sense of humor
- Less concern with order and organization
- A more temperamental nature

Once the gifted child is identified, the teacher must provide a learning environment appropriate to the development of the child's outstanding ability to conceptualize, generalize, create, initiate, relate, organize, and imagine. Chapter 3 contains suggestions for achieving this development.

The teacher should be a facilitator of learning rather than a director of learning. A function of education is to prepare the student for lifelong learning. Every child has an innate curiosity which expands and renews itself in the act of learning. Who has not marveled at the boundless energy and enthusiasm of the bright preschool child as he looks, listens, tastes, smells, and touches everything in sight to satisfy his curiosity? He is open to each new experience and learns from each that which is relevant to his needs. His learning is self-initiated, self-sustaining, and self-satisfying. The act of learning is, in itself, both the result and cause of his increasing curiosity. It is only when the child comes to school that his natural desire to learn is blunted by the imposition of an undifferentiated learning program and a rigid curriculum. Teachers who believe that they must control what a child does, learns, and feels, overlook the built-in drive for learning which resides in each child. If this natural drive is thwarted by the school, the curiosity dies and apathy takes its place. It is only then that external motivation and reward systems are necessary to arouse interest.

The bright child—with his heightened curiosity, wide range of interests, and insight into problems—is particularly thwarted by rigid curriculum requirements. The following suggestions, while appropriate for all children, are vital to the enhancement of lifelong learning habits for gifted children.

1. Build learning experiences around the child's natural curiosity by dealing with problems relevant to his own needs, purposes, and interests.

2. Allow the student to engage in the organization and planning of learning activities.

3. Provide real-life experiences that call for the active participation of the child, and then stress the skills necessary for that participation.

4. Act as a resource for learning rather than as a dispenser of information; resist the temptation to impose knowledge upon a child before he is ready for it.

5. Keep programs flexible enough to encourage exploration and invention.

6. Encourage and reward initiative, inquisitiveness, originality, and a questioning attitude.

7. Allow a child to make his own mistakes and to accept the consequences (as long as the consequences are not dangerous).

One may wonder about the difference between direction and facilitation of learning. It is perhaps a difference in orientation as well as in behavior. Imagine the director standing in front of children and imposing his purposes, desires, and needs upon them; the facilitator stands behind the children and guides them in the realization of their own purposes, desires, and needs. The director imposes assignments, set requirements, and evaluates outcomes; the facilitator supports the students' self-initiated learning and self-determined goals and provides feedback for self-evaluation.

The teacher must provide challenge rather than pressure. The role of the facilitator of learning implies acceptance of the principle that children should be challenged rather than pressured. Because of his initiative and perseverance, the gifted child is particularly receptive to a challenging situation. He enjoys pitting his abilities and experiences against a task that has meaning for him. He doesn't want easy answers. He may even resent being told how to do something because it deprives him of the chance to figure it out for himself. The bright child is far more willing than his less-gifted peer to strike out on his own to explore the difficult and the unknown. He has experienced the exhilaration of accomplishment. This remark is not to suggest that less bright children cannot experience the same exhilaration. The fact is that persistent failure in school makes the less talented child afraid to try. The gifted child is not "turned off" quite so easily.

By the same token, a gifted and creative child is impatient with routine or repetitive assignments. Pressure will not suffice to inspire a child when the teacher views education as the coverage of a body of knowledge. Challenge, on the other hand, gives the child the opportunity to gain confidence in his own powers to think, analyze, organize, and act. The teacher's wise use of questions that ask not only *what* and *when* but *why, how, for what reason, with what intent,* and *to what purpose* aids in challenging a bright student to the kind of thinking that provides the building blocks for speculative theory and philosophy. Assuming that the challenge is appropriate to the child's maturity and experience, it gives him a chance to explore the extent of his powers and to know himself.

The teacher must be as concerned with the process of learning as with the product. In spite of recognition given to an educational philosophy that stresses *learning how to learn,* many teachers act as if education consists of the mastery of a body of knowledge. To make matters worse, educational progress is measured largely through the use of standardized achievement tests which emphasize the acquisition of skills and the memorization of facts. This narrow view of learning is highly undesirable since the abilities involved in recall and application of learned facts are low in the hierarchy of intellectual processes. Much more important to the individual in lifelong learning are the thought processes such as comprehending, analyzing, synthesizing, organizing, and evaluating.

The gifted child is often shortchanged in a system that sees the learner as the passive receiver of knowledge. The gifted child's superior learning ability allows him to score well on most standardized achievement tests, making it appear as though he is doing very well when, in fact, he is failing to develop more than a small fraction of his potential. Emphasis on the following kinds of activities will aid the teacher of gifted children in stressing the importance of the processes of learning rather than the product:

- Problem solving (emphasizing the process rather than the solution)
- Classifying and categorizing
- Comparing and contrasting
- Making judgments according to criteria
- Using resources (dictionaries, encyclopedias, libraries)
- Conducting research projects
- Discussing and debating
- Taking part in class meetings involving group process
- Planning future activities
- Evaluating experiences

In Chapter 3, there are descriptions of programs which have successfully emphasized these processes.

Knowledge of things as they are now becomes obsolete in this world of rapid and inevitable change. The only secure knowledge is the understanding of the processes involved in learning and the ability to apply these processes to new and constantly changing experiences.

The teacher must provide feedback rather than judgment. To become independent and self-reliant adults, children must learn early to evaluate their own learning experiences and achievements. Gifted students are ready for self-assessment and self-evaluation from the time they enter school. It is the job of the teacher to provide feedback information and a behavior model, but the seat of evaluation should be within the child. He should be encouraged to evaluate his own work not in terms of grades and norms but in terms of his own needs, purposes, and goals. Extrinsic evaluation of the child's efforts should be subordinate to intrinsic evaluation. This statement does not mean that the teacher may not evaluate the child's progress and achievement to learn his strengths and weaknesses as a basis for helping him to improve. It does mean, however, that the teacher should refrain from imposing his judgment on the child. Instead of red-penciling and grading a child's composition, the teacher might write a note and point out where the child failed to communicate because of spelling, mechanical, or organizational errors. This approach represents the difference between feedback and judgment.

The teacher must provide alternate learning strategies. One of the most important things a child can learn is that usually there is more than one way to accomplish an objective or attain a goal. There may be several solutions to a problem, several ways of categorizing objects, or several points of view in a discussion. All too often teachers insist that a learning goal be attained in a specified way. Creative children may be quick to point out different strategies which lead to the same outcome. The direct path to a goal may not be the most interesting. Children should be allowed to explore different pathways and even to pause along the way if their interest is captured by a more relevant goal.

For the gifted child who is less creative, alternative learning strategies should be pointed out and demonstrated by the teacher. Creativity is fostered in an atmosphere which provides freedom to experiment. Strategies that are being employed successfully in schools are indicated in Chapter 3.

The teacher must provide a classroom climate which promotes self-esteem and offers safety for creative and cognitive risk-taking. Every child has the right to feel safe to try out novel procedures and to explore new ideas in the classroom (5). The fearful child may consume so much energy in compensating for his repressions and anxieties that he has little energy left to apply to productive and joyful learning. Many creative children are blocked in freedom of expression through fear of criticism, of not pleasing the teacher, of failing, of not being liked, of making mistakes, of being wrong, of not meeting parents' expectations, or by other repressive influences and pressures. New ideas and other forms of divergent response must be welcomed in the classroom which fosters creativity.

Teachers can combat fear by creating a classroom atmosphere in which each child has a sense of belonging, a feeling of self-worth, and a sense of value in his own individuality. How is such an atmosphere created? Some suggestions follow:

- The teacher is supportive and accepting.
- Coercion is not used to manipulate children (i.e. threats about grades, loss of approval, loss of prestige, or banishment).
- The teacher recognizes, accepts, and values individual differences.
- The teacher provides differentiated learning experiences.
- Each child shares in planning his own work and the work of the group.
- The teacher provides enough structure for the child to feel secure but not enough to limit or stifle creative response.
- The teacher accepts and empathizes with strong feelings.
- The teacher recognizes his own limitations.
- The teacher values creativity and welcomes new ideas.

Gifted and creative children are willing to take risks in a warm supportive climate. They will risk the exploration of a new field; they will experiment with different learning techniques; they will share cherished ideas; they will define difficult problems; they will reveal their feelings; they will make mistakes and discover that they can learn from their mistakes; and finally, they will not fear to be themselves.

IMPLICATIONS FOR THE READING PROGRAM

Reading programs for gifted children will deviate in methods, materials, and content utilized; but certain features, such as the following, will be recognized as necessary components of a program for the gifted.

Early assessment of intellectual, perceptual, and reading abilities is vital. Many gifted children learn to read before they come to school, as is pointed out in Chapter 2 of this monograph. This accomplishment is not necessarily the result of formal instruction but rather of a combination of high interest, extraordinary discrimination, and generalizing abilities. Gifted children often discover phonic elements on their own and use context and picture clues readily.

Children who learn to read early may be considered problems when they enter school. Placed with other children in a readiness program or the first preprimer, these gifted children may become bored, restless, and disruptive. Worse, they may withdraw into fantasy to escape the boredom, lose their eagerness to read, and become disillusioned with school in general.

A combination of intelligence and readiness tests, along with careful teacher observation and skill checklists, will give a fair indication of the child's level of competency. The ultimate test is, of course, whether the child can and does read and comprehend written materials.

Gifted children who have not learned to read before school entrance should also be observed carefully since they will be ready to move ahead to advanced work more rapidly than other children. Nothing is more discouraging to the bright, eager child than to be required to persist in drills or activities that are below his level of readiness (9).

The reading program should be highly individualized. With early and accurate assessment of children's abilities, the teacher can individualize the reading program for the gifted child (1). By analyzing his strengths and weaknesses in reading skills, the teacher may decide where the child will profit from instruction with the rest of the group and where he will profit from individual instruction. Each child should be permitted, indeed be encouraged to move ahead as rapidly as he desires and is able to proceed. The reward of accomplishment is a stronger inducement to further effort than we have yet realized.

Care should be taken to assure that the program includes the mastery of skills that provide the foundation for reading growth. Thus, basic word recognition skills should be stressed so that the child gains early independence in reading. It should be noted, however, that phonics, generalizations, and rules of structural analysis are merely tools to aid in word recognition. If it is obvious that the child has achieved independence in word attack and that he is skilled in using the generalizations successfully, then there is no point in continued emphasis and drill on memorizing the rules or practicing their application.

A child should not be discouraged from reading books at higher grade levels than his own. A truly individualized reading program will assess the child's ability at each level and not require him to reread any material that he has read before. It has been suggested that the gifted child's ability to decode sometimes outstrips his ability to comprehend the material he is able to read. It is likely that the child will discontinue efforts to read materials that are not relevant or meaningful to him at some level. Indeed, he may not be able to appreciate the more sophisticated nuances of a selection on first reading. Melville's *Moby Dick* is a prime example of a piece of literature that can be read at different ages with increasing levels of appreciation and understanding. Surely, no one would discourage a youngster from reading the novel because he could not fully grasp Melville's subtle use of symbolism.

The reading program should emphasize development of higher mental processes. Since gifted children attain independence in reading earlier than other students, they also are ready earlier for instruction in inferential, interpretive, and critical reading. Beginning in the primary grades, the gifted will profit from instruction in the following skills:

- Discovering clues from which to infer hidden meanings and probable outcomes
- Analyzing selections to detect author bias and subtle propaganda
- Locating materials on a given topic
- Organizing and synthesizing materials for purposes of reporting
- Evaluating materials in terms of worth and relevancy to purpose
- Understanding the use of connotation, figures of speech, plot, setting, and characterization in reading selections
- Appreciating the motives, intents, and feelings of the author and/or characters in a selection
- Selecting a reading technique and speed appropriate to the difficulty of the material and the purpose for reading it

The reading program should extend interest in reading. The importance of adequate reading skills instruction for the gifted cannot be overstated, but reading is much more than just knowing how to read. The ultimate goal of reading instruction is to establish permanent interest in reading.

An abundance of reading material is required. The voracious reading appetite of the gifted child makes it necessary to provide not only a wide range of materials in terms of variety of subject matter but also material in which in-depth study may be undertaken according to the interests of the student.

It is not enough, however, to provide interesting reading material. Even eager readers need help in choosing books to broaden and enrich their interests as well as to satisfy them. The teacher should become skilled in using child-study techniques, such as an interest inventory, in order to ascertain interests and employ them in the guidance of reading (8). Combining reading with social experience through the use of group projects, play writing and production, creative dramatics, discussion of favorite books, debate of a social issue, and sharing of creative writing broadens reading interests and enriches social relations.

We must be sure that our gifted youth are being provided with the best possible reading instruction not only to develop skill in reading but to nurture a love of learning that guarantees that their education will continue as long as there are good books to read.

REFERENCES

1. Barbe, Walter B. (Ed.). *Psychology and Education of the Gifted: Selected Readings.* New York: Appleton-Century-Crofts, 1965.
2. French, Joseph L. (Ed.). *Educating the Gifted.* New York: Holt, Rinehart and Winston, 1960. (Revised, 1964.)
3. Gallagher, James J. (Ed.). *Teaching Gifted Students: A Book of Readings.* Boston: Allyn and Bacon, 1965.
4. Smith, James A. *Creative Teaching of Reading and Literature in the Elementary School.* Boston: Allyn and Bacon, 1967.
5. Torrance, E. Paul. *Rewarding Creative Behavior.* Englewood Cliffs, New Jersey: Prentice-Hall, 1965.
6. Wittich, M. L. "Innovations in Reading Instruction: For Beginners," in Helen M. Robinson (Ed.), *Innovation and Change in Reading Instruction*, Sixty-seventh Yearbook of the National Society for the Study of Education, Part II. Chicago: University of Chicago Press, 1968.
7. Witty, Paul A. "Who Are the Gifted?" *Education for the Gifted*, Fifty-seventh Yearbook of the National Society for the Study of Education, Part II. Chicago: University of Chicago Press, 1958.
8. Witty, Paul A., Alma M. Freeland, and Edith H. Grotberg. *The Teaching of Reading.* Boston: D.C. Heath, 1966.
9. Witty, Paul A. *Helping the Gifted Child.* Chicago: Science Research Associates, 1952. (Revised with Edith H. Grotberg, 1970.)

CHAPTER 6

A Look Ahead in the Education of the Gifted and the Creative

Paul A. Witty

EDUCATION HAS COME to be regarded by many persons as a process through which the maximum development of every child is sought in accord with his unique nature and needs. This concept is in harmony with democratic ideals since in a democracy each citizen contributes to the common welfare to the extent of his ability. To enable every person to make his greatest contribution, we should offer individually stimulating and suitable educational opportunities.

Educators have awakened to the fact that too often gifted children have been neglected in our schools. These children have seldom been sufficiently challenged to develop their unusual abilities. Special funds have, of course, been appropriated for the education of the disadvantaged, the mentally retarded, the physically handicapped, and the disabled pupil; but little special provision has been made for the gifted. As a result, children of superior ability are often "left to develop their own skills in their own way and in terms of personal initiative alone" (2). In spite of this situation, some gifted pupils progress desirably. Others, however, in large numbers fail to achieve their youthful promise. Of all groups of exceptional children, perhaps the most neglected is the gifted. For years, surveys have made it clear that the typical elementary and secondary school provides a too-restricted offering. In many schools today, the abilities of gifted children are unrecognized; and in others, they are unchallenged or neglected.

That teacher-training institutions are doing little to cultivate appreciation of the needs of the gifted is generally evident. Moreover, professional educators and school personnel are failing to provide materials and methods that are more than token gestures in the education of the gifted. Inclusion of this topic in books and curricula for teacher education is rare. Even in the professional literature on the teaching of reading and in books on the education of the gifted, discussion of the topic of reading for the gifted is conspicuously meager or absent, as is shown in Chapters 2 and 3. A cooperative effort should be made to develop more effective teacher training programs.

That the neglect of the gifted is even more acute today than in the past may be seen by examining very recent surveys. In *Ac'cent on Talent,* two surveys are cited by Bryan and Lewis (1). It was found in 1963 that only thirteen states employed full-time State Department of Education members who were responsible for the education of the gifted. Despite persistent efforts to obtain increased opportunities, it was disclosed some five years later, that there were only twelve states with full-time personnel assigned to the gifted. Moreover, the definition of the gifted pupil is often limited to children of high IQ, and more inclusive current definitions are seldom considered.

As indicated in Chapter 2, perhaps the most useful definition of the gifted holds that a gifted child is one whose performance in a worthwhile type of human endeavor is consistently or repeatedly remarkable. We observed the inefficiency of intelligence tests to identify creative persons and suggested that samples of behavior be used and evaluated in efforts to discover pupils of promise in areas such as art, music, writing, dramatics, and social leadership. Similar conclusions were reached concerning the practical worth of tests of creativity which have been criticized repeatedly for their lack of validity and reliability. Although progress is being made in developing more valid tests, it seems desirable, at present, to rely primarily on other approaches in the identification of the creative person. In Chapter 3, several "operational" approaches which are being successfully used are described.

Indicated in Chapter 2 are some of the outstanding characteristics of gifted and creative pupils. It was observed that perhaps half of the verbally gifted pupils who have been the subjects of genetic studies learned to read before entering school. These children usually had rich and varied opportunities for early learning in homes in which reading and language development were respected and fostered. Such opportunities undoubtedly have a favorable influence on children's acquisition of reading skills. Investigators have recently demonstrated that with appropriate opportunities and motivation, children of varied backgrounds can learn to read during the preschool years. In fact, studies suggest that opportunities to learn to read may prove suitable and rewarding for many children at age four.

Experimentation is needed to explore further the role of early learning in affecting intelligence, as well as in fostering reading and language skills. The possibilities, at present, are great also for constructive research in which the components of creative performance are identified and examined critically in so far as worthwhile or productive performance is concerned. It should be borne in mind that *divergent* behavior is not tantamount to productive and worthwhile creative endeavor since *divergent* behavior can be either destructive and detrimental to social welfare or constructive and rewarding. Criteria for desirable goals should be established by research.

Programs to engender various kinds of creativity are infrequently found in our schools. Increasing numbers of teachers are to be commended, however, for their efforts to foster the expression and development of creativity in their classrooms. Moreover, some progress is being made in the formulation of criteria. For example, Walter (4) has presented some outstanding children's poems and has set forth criteria for evaluation. It will prove rewarding for teachers and administrators to examine practical suggestions of Torrance and Wilson (3, 5) concerning the form of procedures and activities designed to help the child practice the creative process.

It has become clear that the gifted child needs individually suitable and interesting reading experiences from the beginning of his school entrance (6). If he is able to read on entering kindergarten or first grade, he should be encouraged to do so from varied sources that are individually challenging and appealing. In every class, opportunities should be provided and guidance offered so that the gifted pupil will continue to develop his reading abilities and to apply them widely.

In many reading programs, little attention is given to interest and motivation. It is gratifying, nevertheless, to find some classroom teachers planning programs of reading and language instruction designed to enable gifted pupils to follow and develop worthwhile interests. A few such programs are noted in Chapter 3. In these programs the teacher often works closely with the school librarian. They study interests and needs by appropriate techniques, such as an interest inventory, and assist pupils in obtaining the right books. Enrichment programs of these kinds are sometimes associated with related efforts designed to help the gifted pupil to satisfy his personal and social needs through reading and to find joy in reading. In addition, experiences in reading are correlated with activities in writing, oral expression, and other aspects of the language arts (7).

It is almost inconceivable that educators and citizens have permitted the longstanding neglect of gifted and creative children and youth to persist. There are, however, some current trends and practices in education that are heartening as correctives. There are programs throughout the United States, such as those described in Chapter 3, which are planned specifically for the gifted and creative youth. The programs presently stand as examples of the best that education can offer. Increasingly, dedicated teachers are recognizing individual differences and are practicing personalized instruction for gifted children which will satisfy varied interests and needs. Nongraded or continuous development programs are designed also to permit the gifted pupil as well as others to progress steadily according to differences in ability and accomplishment. Moreover, varied resources in the forms of new-type textbooks, programed instruction, and audiovisual materials are being more widely used to care for individual differences. All these approaches encourage the extension and enrichment of opportunities for the gifted and the creative pupil and also provide more adequate and stimulating experiences for the disadvantaged. Thus, by increased attention to individual differences, gifted and creative pupils are becoming the recipients of much needed opportunities and enrichment although it must be recognized that the total provision is small and there is need for more developmental reading programs designed to care for the full range of pupil abilities and aptitudes.

The present needs of the gifted and the creative pupil are acute, and carefully planned provisions are needed now. It is hoped that this monograph will stimulate teachers and administrators to give increased attention to this problem and will lead them to undertake more widespread efforts in behalf of the gifted and talented student. By extending and enriching opportunities in the area of reading, educators can make a significant contribution.

REFERENCES

1. Bryan, J. Ned, and Lanora G. Lewis. "Are State Departments Failing to Provide Leadership for the Gifted?" *Ac'cent on Talent—An NEA Service to Schools of the Nation,* 2 (May 1968), 7-8.

2. Miles, Catherine C. "Gifted Children," in Leonard Carmichael (Ed.), *Manual of Child Psychology.* New York: John Wiley and Sons, 1946, 931.

3. Torrance, E. P. *Gifted Children in the Classroom.* New York: Macmillan, 1965.

4. Walter, Nina W. *Let Them Write Poetry.* New York: Holt, Rinehart and Winston, 1962.

5. Wilson, Robert C. "Creativity," *Education for the Gifted,* Fifty-seventh

Yearbook of the National Society for the Study of Education, Part II. Chicago: University of Chicago Press, 1958, Chapter Six.

6. Witty, Paul A. "A Balanced Reading Program for the Gifted," *Reading Teacher,* 16 (May 1963).

7. Witty, Paul A., Alma M. Freeland, and Edith H. Grotberg. *The Teaching of Reading.* Boston: D.C. Heath, 1966.